Pastoral Care
Essentials

12 KEYS TO ENHANCE YOUR PASTORAL CARE

CWR
Andy Peck

Contents

Introduction

Picking up this book implies that you are interested in the subject of pastoral care. Maybe it's an area of serving that you want to learn more about. Maybe it's a ministry that your church is already engaged with but where there might be room for improvement. In this book, we will be looking at what pastoral care means; why it may struggle in certain churches; biblical approaches to care; developing a vision; and suggesting solutions and structures for your church. By reflecting on what God calls all of us to do and with a little thought, energy and adjustment, pastoral care systems can be designed in a way that will reflect His love and grace to others.

If you are involved in pastoral care, or aspire to be, hopefully this book will give you some fresh ideas or at least assure you that you are on the right track. If you are in church leadership, you might gain some new approaches to translate into your church. These might take a little while to implement but, coupled with a genuine desire to care for people, you may soon discover that people grow in their faith, and the church has capacity to expand its care beyond its walls.

The contents of this book are based on courses I have written and run at CWR over the last 12 years. Most have been delivered at Waverley Abbey House, some 'on the road' at various locations in England. I would particularly like to thank my former colleague, Ron Kallmier, whose wisdom, experience and insight was such a help when I first started leading pastoral care courses. I'd also like to thank the many students whose feedback and input have helped to earth and improve the material as the years have gone by.

The book is structured into three parts: essential understanding, essential practice and essential strategy. You can, of course, focus on the areas that interest you, but I recommend that you read chapters 1 and 2 first to establish what is understood by the term 'pastoral care'.

Hopefully, you will find some nuggets in each chapter to help you progress in this vital area of church ministry.

Part 1

Essential understanding

 **01:** **Decide to improve**

Geraint Thomas' win of the Tour de France in 2018 continued an astonishingly successful period for British cycling and Team Ineos (previously known as Team Sky). Since 2012, when Bradley Wiggins became the first British cyclist to win the Tour de France, a Team Ineos rider has won the race five out of six years (Chris Froome won four times). British cycling had been something of a joke for decades but was suddenly at the pinnacle of the sport.

Team Ineos' ability to sign up the best cyclists has something to do with their success, but many cycling analysts believe that the appointment of Dave Brailsford as performance director for British Cycling in 2003 was the catalyst to this meteoric rise. His approach was to stand back and ask: how could they improve cycling performance by 1%? He believed that aggregating marginal gains would lead to significant success.

Some of these small improvements included: redesigning the bike seats to make them more comfortable; rubbing alcohol on the tyres for a better grip; and giving riders electrically heated over shorts to wear to maintain ideal muscle temperature. Brailsford even had different types of massage gels tested to see which one led to the fastest muscle recovery, and hired a surgeon to teach the cyclists the best way to wash their hands to reduce the chances of catching a cold. We cannot be sure how much these elements paid off in Team Ineos' success individually, but Brailsford's eye for detail was clearly relevant.

Those involved in pastoral care ministry will be best placed to see where 'marginal gains' could happen, and have the influence to implement necessary change. It is not difficult to list areas of improvement but this work needs to be done at a number of levels. A key decision is making sure that the right approach is adopted.

As the book unfolds, we will explore what is meant by 'pastoral care' and how we can model Jesus in the way we care.

Reasons why pastoral care is struggling in some churches

The sole pastor model might not be working

In many churches, the model for pastoral care is the pastor, vicar or church leader caring for the whole congregation. Their primary job is seen as providing care for both church members and those on the fringe of church life. Initially, a church leader may be willing to assume this additional role out of necessity but then struggle to hand over this responsibility to someone else. In addition, church members may be reluctant to take over a job previously done by the pastor. However, most ministers do not have the time or energy to solely create a healthy pastoral culture so that everyone grows in faith. Indeed, in most parts of the world, pastors are bi-vocational. They may have another full or part-time role in addition to being a church pastor.

The rationale behind a sole pastor model has been developed

through a mixture of church history and understanding of the Bible. One famed advocate of this approach was Richard Baxter, whose ministry to his church in Kidderminster in the seventeenth century saw many hundreds come to faith. As well as preaching on Sundays and midweek, his practice was to systematically visit his parishioners from house to house, explaining basic doctrine and enquiring after their spiritual life. For many, this was a typical and lauded approach: the person deemed the spiritual head of the church responsible for the life and wellbeing of the congregation. His book charting his pastoral approach, *The Reformed Pastor*[1], is highly regarded.

Advocates of the sole pastor model believe that the plural of 'pastors' in Ephesians 4:11 is referring to a number of sole pastors. They also see Paul's pastoral epistles (1 Timothy, 2 Timothy and Titus) as a template for how pastors should operate.

There have certainly been many excellent men and women who have served their churches as the sole pastoral carer. However, I don't believe that the Bible advocates the idea that one person should bear the whole burden of pastoral care. (We will look at this in more detail in chapter 3.)

Conclusion: perhaps we need to rethink our model of pastoral care in the local church.

Many serving as pastors are struggling

The New Testament often refers to pastors and leaders in the plural, and it is not surprising why the burden of being a sole pastor is too much, and why many decide to leave the role.

In 2018, The Good Book Company published results of an online survey, completed by almost 500 people, which investigated working patterns and stress among those in paid Christian work. The survey revealed that:

- Christians in ministry, particularly those on part-time contracts, regularly work double the number of hours officially required.
- Around 15% of people surveyed reported working over 70 hours a week, placing them firmly in the zone of increased risks to both mental and physical health.
- Almost half of those surveyed do not regularly have a day off a week.
- One third of survey respondents have experienced burnout.
- Two thirds of those surveyed are meeting with friends or others who might support them only intermittently.
- About 80% of people surveyed feel guilty that they are letting people down by not doing a good job.
- Over half of respondents have had some experience of feeling worthless and believing themselves to be unsuited to their ministry role.

> 'Even accounting for potential bias in those who chose to fill in the survey, this is a shocking level of illness relating to ministry... People are zealous to do gospel work, and are often working unsupervised and unsupported, but under the critical eye of members of the congregation. People will regularly push through the tiredness or keep going on adrenaline and coffee, only to crash badly at some stage.' (Tim Thornborough)[2]

Supporters of the sole pastor approach might argue that these finding don't invalidate the model, but it's no surprise that most people cannot cope with a role that was never intended to rest on one person alone. Pastoral ministry was always intended to be plural, with ministry shared across a number of folk.

Conclusion: we need a clear understanding of the role of pastoral care workers.

The complexity of pastoral needs has increased

The level and complexity of needs within churches has always been high: people get sick, lose jobs, fall out with each other and struggle spiritually. A church might be faced with a range of additional challenges: eating disorders, addictions, relational needs, mental health and debt – as well as issues regarding marriage, sexual identity, parenting, and caring for the elderly. In more recent decades, loneliness has increased because of family break up, and financial pressures on social services has led to increased strain on those people who are in need of support.

Of course, healthcare provision, especially in the UK, is available, and in many cases, parishioners would make an appointment with a doctor rather than the reverend – but many see that the role of the pastor is to 'care for the flock' and so bring their issue to him or her. Many ministers may be ill equipped for that role but feel obliged to have an answer to every dilemma.

I entered pastoral ministry naïvely assuming that the expectation was that I would be a faithful teacher of the Bible, only to discover that a pastor is also seen as: a counsellor, a social worker, a marriage guidance specialist, a manager of volunteers, a negotiator, a business manager and a caretaker. And if you are judged as not competent, you will be told that you are not up to the job!

Conclusion: we need manageable expectations to handle human need.

The pastoral needs are overwhelming

Not only are the needs complex, but situations requiring pastoral care come thick and fast; for example, a girl with an eating disorder, an aged women with dementia, a person with an addiction to porn, a young lad you fear may be being abused, and a couple on the leadership team who are considering breaking up – and that's just people with care needs on Monday!

In the animated film *Fantasia*[3], there is a segment called 'The Sorcerer's Apprentice' where Mickey Mouse attempts to use magic to speed up his cleaning, but it goes spectacularly wrong. He eventually has numerous multiplying brooms spilling buckets of water everywhere. No sooner has he dealt with one broom, than another one appears in a nightmarish scene. Pastoral care can have that feel. Some issues are just developing while others are finally being resolved. Most seem to appear from nowhere. In some cases, it's pretty clear what is required; in others, you start to base a solution on one problem only to discover that the actual problem is something else, which you are pretty sure you cannot solve. Added to the mix is that sometimes the offered care is misunderstood or deemed unhelpful, and so the carer themselves is faced with the injustice of being a target when their motivation for involvement was to provide a solution.

Issues rarely arrive at a convenient time, and the mix of interrelationship dynamics can be tricky to navigate, especially in a closely knit church community. The better you are at helping people, the more people will want to see you. As a church reaches out, they inevitably find people whose level of need exceeds their capacity to cope, and so it continues.

Conclusion: we need an approach that recognises the vastness of the need.

Pastoral ministry can lose focus on Christ's mandate to make disciples

This book's definition of pastoral care is drawn from Jesus, whose chief concern is that we become followers of Him. Too often, however, pastoral ministry is a reaction to issues, and fails to help the person in their walk with Christ. No doubt each of the apostles could have functioned as a traditional pastor type but that would have meant failing to fulfil the commands that Jesus left them with: to pass on the faith in order that others become devoted followers of Jesus.

Neil Hudson wrote in *Imagine Church*[4] of the need for some leaders to 'renegotiate the contract with the church'. He discovered that the missional disciple-making role he believed he needed to exercise contrasted with the more pastoral role that his church wanted from him. The gap in expectations needed addressing. Many church attendees don't actually want to be too much like Jesus, and so there may be initial resistance when a church leader starts getting serious. People may even leave a church if disciple-making is put on the agenda.

Conclusion: we need pastoral care to include the whole person, not just the presenting need.

The structure of the sole pastor model is inward looking

You may well have noticed that church attendance in the UK is not encouraging. Church attendance has declined from 6,484,300 in 1980 to 3,081,500 according to data collected in 2015 (equivalent to a decline from 11.8% to 5% of the total UK population)[5]. Church attendance dwindles for a whole host of reasons and it would be stretching the point to suggest that the pastor-centric approach to pastoral care is a major factor. After all, there have been many churches that would attribute their growth to the appointment of one particular pastor. Generally speaking, churches appoint pastors to lead the church and to look after the flock. On occasions, someone gifted as an evangelist might be in the role (while still being referred to as 'pastor') and equipped and able to help the church grow, but that would perhaps be the exception. Good pastoral care (we will define this later) is an important ingredient in sustaining church life, encouraging church growth and, practised biblically, can be a vital part of church growth. Looking at most churches in the UK at present, however, you will find that those led by sole pastors have a bigger challenge in making evangelism a priority than those with team leadership. Sheep bleat; fish don't make a sound. Very few pastors have had a non-believer (fish) phone them to ask about the Christian faith, but you can be sure that he or she will have had calls from believers (sheep) asking for help.

Consider this: many churches see no growth whatsoever. One US study suggested that it 'costs' $1,500[6] for every person added to the church. In other words, if the purpose of the church is to 'make disciples' and you were to measure the 'disciple making output' from financial resources, then you could see how much money is spent by churches in getting one person to come to church.

Some churches have unwritten dos and don'ts regarding their minister. A new pastor enters into pastoral ministry and the subtle expectation from church members might be: 'You may dedicate (or baptise) our children, marry us, visit us when we are sick and bury us. Just don't challenge us too much!'

Clearly this is way off the mandate that Jesus gave, which made no mention at all about marrying, visiting and burying, but did tell us to make disciples (Matt. 28:19). Structure, whether sole pastor approach or otherwise, is not the only factor in church growth. Churches that grow will have given someone with an outward focus room to move. This may be a volunteer, if a church doesn't have funds for more than one full-time church leader, or another member of staff.

Conclusion: we need to ensure that our focus is not preventing church growth.

Many churches cannot support a full-time person

The sole pastor approach is not ideal for the reasons listed, but you will know that many churches cannot afford to appoint a paid minister anyway. Worldwide there are more bi-vocational pastors than sole pastors, but even in the west, where there are more paid ministers, most local churches cannot afford the kind of model promoted.

According to figures from UK Church Statistics 2005–2015, there were 36,636 ministers in 2010 for the UK's 50,709 churches – 1.38 churches to every minister[7].

Some denominations, mostly Anglicans and Methodists, share ministers across several churches; whereas other denominations, especially people in some of the new church streams, are taking more part-time ministers.

Across the whole country and all denominations, the median size of a church is 44 people. So there are almost 20,000 churches with less than 44 on a Sunday. Attendance across the 5% smallest churches is seven people and across the 25% smallest churches it is 15[8]. Many of these churches will have some pastoral support, as ministers serve more than one congregation. Some of these smaller churches are in rural areas, and they will be one of a number of churches the vicar serves. If the model is: 'find a pastor' to care for the flock, many local churches are shepherd-less.

Conclusion: we need approaches that don't depend on a full-time worker.

Churches are struggling to find carers

If a church is not able to appoint a paid pastoral carer then one solution would be to appoint volunteers to assist those who are in a full-time role. But such is the challenge of pastoral ministry, there is a reluctance to come forward. Many are facing enough challenges at home and work of their own, never mind other people's problems. If you are running on empty, you are wise not to make any more emotional journeys that might bring you to a juddering halt. Look at most pastoral care teams and many of those who have capacity to serve will be women (yes, even in these egalitarian days this is still the norm), or people who are retired.

Conclusion: we need a care process that doesn't just depend on the free time of a few brave souls.

Care is often haphazard and ill judged

Even if a church has pastoral carers, sometimes it is haphazard in the way it supports and deploys those who volunteer.

Take the following issues:
- A homeless man comes to the church seeking money.
- A same-sex couple want to have their baby blessed.
- A husband and father of three children, and a regular church member, has a heart attack in the garden and dies in the ambulance.

- A young lad complains of bullying by the youth worker.
- A newly married couple are having difficulties in their relationship and need counselling.
- A member of the church has just had a third miscarriage.

Each issue will have its complexities. Some (maybe all) require pastoral care from someone.

Assuming you are on the pastoral care team, would you know what to do in each? Have you thought through scenarios so you know what kind of action to take? What procedures will you adopt to ensure that God's grace is brought to the areas of need?

If we are making decisions on the run, in times of crisis, we are less well-placed than if we prayerfully consider an approach that connects with the ethos of the church and the gifts of the caring team.

Conclusion: we need a considered approach if we are to be even-handed in our care.

Those in need are not expressing their needs

Most of us, if we are in acute pain, will be vocal and desperate in seeking any help we can. Others might be suffering quietly with less obvious or urgent needs.

All of us are on a process of growth towards being more like Christ and anything that gets in the way needs to be addressed. Sometimes, it requires courage to seek assistance, and we only do so if there is a strong likelihood of things improving. A person's need might not be a serious illnesses or major crises but pains and fears that are buried; burdens that are carried around, slowing their progress and diminishing their efforts. Unless there is a widespread culture of sharing needs and finding approaches and solutions, people will simply suffer in silence. Better to keep quiet than have hopes of respite or recovery dashed.

Conclusion: we need to create a caring culture that includes everyone.

Moving on

If riding a bike race is deemed worthy of a little work looking at marginal gains, how much more the people of God and the kingdom of God? Maybe you recognise some of these issues in your church? I would like to invite you to be part of a revolution that sees churches improving their pastoral care and sees not just marginal gains, but major gains.

In this book, we will look at what Scripture has to say about areas of pastoral care. There might not be an exact blueprint to follow, but there are principles that will guide us to wise pathways for our particular congregation, or pastoral care environment. Above all, I hope this book will improve your understanding of pastoral care and how to structure that care.

In the past, I have struggled with perfectionist tendencies and was intrigued to read in a time management book that perfectionism is spelt: P A R A L Y S I S. These tendencies were, at times, stopping me getting things done. I feared making a mistake, not being prepared, or not taking sufficient care.

You may look at pastoral care in your church and see lots of areas for improvement, or maybe too much. You might fear starting to implement changes because you might not succeed. But I would encourage you to do what you can. Aim high by all means but don't let the size of the task daunt you. Doing something can help you make that 1% improvement, which, together with other improvements, may make a lasting difference in the lives of people inside and outside the church.

[1] Richard Baxter, *The Reformed Pastor* (CreateSpace Independent Publishing Platform, 2011)
[2] Rachel Jones, 'Could your pastor be close to burnout? Our survey says yes', March 2016, taken from thegoodbook.co.uk [Accessed March 2019]
[3] *Fantasia*, Walt Disney Studios, 1940
[4] Neil Hudson, *Imagine Church* (London: IVP, 2012)
[5] Peter Brierley, Future First, Issue 53, October 2017, taken from brierleyconsultancy.com [Accessed March 2019]
[6] Sam Hailes, 'Profile: Francis Chan', Premier Christianity, February 2019, p24
[7] Peter Brierley, *UK Church Statistics, 2005–2015* (Tonbridge: ADBC Publishers, 2011) p136
[8] Statistics for Mission 2016, p9, taken from churchofengland.org [Accessed April 2019]

02: Know what pastoral care is really about

You are no doubt familiar with the story of the child in Sunday school who, when asked, 'What's grey and furry and gathers nuts in winter?' replied, 'Well, it sounds like a squirrel to me, but we are in Sunday school, so I expect the answer is – Jesus!'

When we ask the question, 'What is pastoral care, according to the Bible?' The answer is – Jesus. The word 'pastoral' is derived from the Latin word meaning shepherd. This farming metaphor, common in the land of Israel, became a word associated with the kings of Israel whose role was to rule and lead Israel wisely. David worked as a shepherd before his unlikely selection to be king and was the Hebrew poster boy of the ideal ruler. The hope was (and is for Jews today) that a David-like king might one day return Israel to its former glory. So when Jesus said, 'I am the good shepherd' (John 10:11), He was contrasting His perfect care for people with the imperfect care of leaders, past and present. In the last chapter, we reflected on how the quality and focus of pastoral care in many churches is short of what it could be, and hinted at some of the reasons. In this chapter, we will see that Jesus is the perfect shepherd/pastor for His people, and also a model of how to care for others.

Throughout the New Testament, the writers acknowledge that Jesus is the 'Chief Shepherd' (1 Pet. 5:4), who, as Lord of all, continues to lead His Church. If we believe the Bible to be true but are pastoring differently to Jesus, it's not really pastoral care.

How does Jesus care for us?

Imagine you have a bad gash on your leg – you would go straight to Accident and Emergency and hope that they will deal with your need. If they give you paracetamol and turn you away without stitching up the wound, you would be rightly aggrieved. Your need was not met.

If you were granted a positive answer to prayer for one need, what would that need be? The truth is that whatever need we bring, God has already provided the remedy to humanity's chief need: reconciliation with Himself, without which we are estranged from our maker and unable to enjoy all He has for us in this life and the life to come. We know that this came at an immense cost – the life, death and resurrection of Jesus. This was the culmination of God's plan to bless the world through the people of Israel who had so far failed in their task to be a light to the nations. Jesus came to rescue His people. He dealt with the pain of our eternal separation from God. He dealt a fatal blow to the powers of darkness and will one day bring us to a place where we will know the deepest joy and freedom from pain for eternity. It's hard to overemphasise the importance of that sentence. Has anyone cared more than Jesus?

We can compare Jesus to the Passover lamb (John 19:14; 1 Cor. 5:7). Just as the death of a lamb and the sprinkling of blood led to freedom for the Israelites of old from oppression in Egypt, His death would lead to freedom for Israel, and all who place their faith in that act, from the oppression of sin.

The resurrection of Jesus is the proof that God the Father accepted the sacrifice and opens up the way for humanity to know resurrection life, so that physical death is not the end for them, but a gateway into the new heavens and earth.

The apostle Paul, reflecting on Jesus, said that God showed the extent of His love for us, in that 'while we were still sinners,' (rebelling against our maker) 'Christ died for us' (Rom. 5:8). Jesus did all that was necessary for us to be made whole again and, as the victorious Lord of all, has been given a position of authority at the pinnacle of the universe. In Christ, we can know hearts that are cleansed, forgiveness of sin and peace with God. This is the deluxe premium care package available for all.

The truths of this familiar gospel message can be forgotten amidst the pressing needs that seem so immediate. If the cure for someone in your care who had a disease was in your medicine cabinet, you wouldn't hesitate to give it to them. Similarly, if you claim to care for someone, you would want them to know that their true need has been met in Christ. Your need and mine is wonderfully met through Jesus, so that we can say: 'I live by faith in the Son of God, who loved me and gave himself for me' (Gal. 2:20).

Living in the kingdom

Given the importance of Jesus' death and resurrection, His sole message could have been: 'Hey guys, I am going to die for your sin and rise from the dead in the future. When it happens, put your trust in me!' But it wasn't. He begins His three-year public ministry with a neat summary of His message: "'The time has come," he said. "The kingdom of God has come near. Repent and believe the good news!"' (Mark 1:14–15).

Jesus is inviting the nation of Israel back to God by using kingdom of God language they would have known, but giving it a new twist. The phrase 'kingdom of God' evoked images of when their nation had a king who reigned from Jerusalem and had overcome all their enemies – the halcyon days. Jesus explains that now God's kingdom has no spatial boundaries. The kingdom of the rule and reign of God had begun but it required His listeners, and us today, to change patterns of thinking (repent) and live in the good of it (believe) – in other words, live as if this is true.

In 2005, stories came to light of two Japanese men, Yoshio Yamakawa (87) and Tsuzuki Nakauchi (85), who were former soldiers in a division of the Japanese army whose ranks had been devastated in fierce battles with US forces towards the end of the Second World War. These men had deserted their post and hidden on the island of Mindanao, which is 600 miles from Manila, Philippines. Afraid that they might be court martialled for desertion, the men were apparently unaware that the war was over. Here were two men hiding in guilt and shame during a period of peace and freedom.

Jesus invites us to live in the good of the kingdom, which is here. All we need to do is step out into the light. The war is over. God's kingdom has come. In the Gospels, Jesus explains the values of the kingdom that He is inviting people into. It would affect everything about our lives: how we speak, how we think, how we act, how we handle sexual desire, what we do with our money, and so on. Jesus also introduces us to God, but this time as a Father. God is the very best kind of dad. You can trust Him to look after you, be rooting for you and, yes, caring for you.

To convey how radical living in the kingdom would be, Jesus used a shocking metaphor that was sadly familiar to the people in Roman occupied Israel. He said that following Him meant taking up our cross, referencing the vile practice that the Romans used to execute people. Jesus was saying – say goodbye to your old life and embrace this new one. But don't try to live both at the same time. Just as a single person says goodbye to singleness when they marry, or a civilian says goodbye to their freedom when they enrol in the army, so we embrace the fact that He calls the shots on how we live. How does it work out when a newlywed tries to liaise with old flames? Or how does a soldier get on when he goes AWOL when he's supposed to be in barracks? Not well. We can't truly follow Jesus unless other approaches to living are firmly kicked into touch.

Jesus' care is not just for the life to come, as many have supposed: an insurance policy for the afterlife; but for the way we live now. We see this especially in His work with the Twelve disciples. These were men who were with Him 24/7. (Although an odd practice now, this would have been more usual in that day when religious leaders would typically have disciples who would listen and imitate their practice.) Jesus' call to be His apprentice would have been exciting and intriguing for the original Twelve, many of whom would have assumed that their school days were behind them. Some of their classmates had already gone on to further education and a few had become disciples of the iterant rabbis who showed up in the village. Most had dropped out of school aged 12 and took up the profession of their father, which for many (eg Peter, Andrew, James and John) was fishing. Now here's this man, rumoured to be the Messiah, inviting them to be His disciples. This is sort of equivalent to a university professor inviting a teenager to research a doctorate, when they haven't yet passed their GCSEs. I say 'sort of' because this is an apprenticeship that requires activity, not noses in books in dusty libraries. A disciple would literally become like his rabbi. (Sorry, the male pronoun is deliberate: women weren't allowed to be disciples.)

Jesus was leading these men to know God within the kingdom just as He Himself knew God. This meant teaching vital life-changing material, but also revealing what knowing God was like. Most people know that Jesus was a miracle worker, and can probably come up with a few examples from the 37 or so detailed in the Gospels. But few link these miracles as being part of the kingdom message that Jesus and the apostles preached. The blind see, the lame walk, the deaf hear, the demon possessed are released. The conditions of heaven are coming to earth. The powers of the age to come are entering this present world. So in the Gospels, Jesus invites people into the rule of God. His care for His people involves teaching them life in the kingdom and then demonstrating the power of that kingdom.

A typical week as a disciple of Jesus would probably have involved being 'astonished' (Matt. 22:33) by His teaching, laughing at His choice of imagery (Matt. 19:24), and being asked to do some challenging things like wandering into villages announcing the kingdom and healing the sick. If someone had asked the disciples, 'How does Jesus care for you?' They might have replied, 'Well, the whole experience of learning from Him is a kind of care. I am learning how to live better. My conscience is clean. I have a sense of purpose. When I mess up, I know what to do. I am being stretched, in a good way, to accomplish stuff for God. Things that I read about in the Scriptures (Old Testament), I have seen with my own eyes.'

The Gospels do not give us much detail on the personal interactions between Jesus and the Twelve, so we have to assume that what we have in the Gospels is all we need to be followers ourselves today. In the Great Commission (Matt. 28:18–20), Jesus tells His remaining eleven disciples to make more followers by immersing them in the power and love of the triune God and teaching others what they had learnt from Him.

It is very hard for us, with 2,000 years of church history, to return in our minds to what Jesus actually said and taught. We have all the trappings of modern church life: buildings and stained glass windows, purpose-built auditoriums, or school halls where the church gathers. We have a variety of styles of church leader: some who wear robes, some who don't, some with titles, some paid and some bi-vocational. We have church schools, charities, conferences and a wealth of Christian resources. And we have Christians involved in caring organisations that are not strictly 'Christian', such as the National Health Service.

The focus of the early Christians, after Jesus had ascended to His Father, was to keep in step with the Holy Spirit in what He was looking for them to do in Jerusalem, the surrounding area and then further afield. When someone embraced the good news of Jesus, the apostles' care of them would be to help them understand His teaching, so that they can help their family and friends to live in the kingdom too.

Of course, because Jesus is no less Lord in heaven then when He lived on earth, He can still be asked to perform the miracles that He performed in His earthly ministry. Jesus Himself had predicted that the disciples would do greater works than Him, a phrase variously interpreted, but suggests that, post Jesus' earthly life, miracles would not be less impressive. When Luke writes about the Early Church, he seems at pains to record similar miracles happening then to those that Jesus had performed; for example, Peter and Paul raising the dead.

If you had been in Jerusalem on a Sunday and wandered down to where the first Christians met for worship, you would have found them keen to engage with you, check whether you were enjoying the good news for yourself and, doubtless, have offered to pray with you about anything you mentioned that was not currently working out as God's will on earth as in heaven.

Living in the kingdom connects the wonderful truth of Christ's death and resurrection to our daily life. It's actually all intended to be part of the same thing. When we come to Him, we die to self and know new life in Him, born again of the Spirit of God and live a new kind of life following in His way in the kingdom, now and until the day when (through death or His return) we finally enjoy the new heavens and new earth.

Jesus' model of pastoral care and implications

There is no division between pastoral care and evangelism
Jesus engaged with everyone and introduced them to the kingdom of God, inviting them to enter by following in His way. This requires turning from their wisdom to embrace His. If we are aiming to care for someone, this needs to be our paramount concern too. Of course, if a person is in physical pain, sharing the gospel is not our first action, but if we follow Jesus' model of caring then we don't just deal with the physical needs and never look to share anything else. Remember Jesus' interaction with the

man whose friends lowered him through the roof on a stretcher (Luke 5:17–26)? Jesus enabled this lame man to walk, but also forgave his sins, knowing that though the presenting need was failure to walk, his real need was failure to be right with God.

Sometimes, people might be manifestly uninterested in the good news and we need to recognise when to back off. However, it might be the ideal opportunity to tactfully offer God's unconditional love and minister, in Christ's name, in a way that is respectful of them in their stage of the journey. Let's *share* the good news as well as *be* good news.

Jesus cares for the whole life

Jesus healed all who came to Him. There are only two recorded incidences where He seemed to delay healing: when He delayed visiting His sick friend, Lazarus, because He knew that, at the right time, He would raise him from the dead, and when He seemed to initially tease the Syro-Phonecian woman before healing her daughter (Mark 7:24–30). These examples aside, everyone who came to Jesus, expressing a need for healing, went away blessed.

If Jesus is our model of pastoral care, then we might find that a tad daunting. We might feel uncomfortable praying for healing, or are unsure that it would be successful because we have not had much experience of this in our own church. That's understandable and most of us are on a journey regarding praying for healing. I certainly had long periods in my Christian life when this kind of talk freaked me out.

But praying for healing is a wonderful example of the potential of pastoral care. When we pray, we know that there is nothing we can *do* to effect change. We are merely seeking to tap into the power provided by the risen Jesus. Our trust in Him becomes a conduit for heavenly resources just as a doctor might access the medical resources of the NHS. We have been given authority to do this, just as a doctor has authority. And we leave the need with Him. If they are healed, we rejoice. If they are partially healed, we pray some more. If they are not healed, we promise to go on praying and assure them that God dearly loves them.

Depending on God to respond to our prayers in power can be vital as we seek to care. As we speak loving words of sympathy, share a thought, remind them of God's love, listen to their needs, we do so knowing that without Jesus we 'can do nothing' (John 15:5).

Jesus cares by teaching

In Romans chapter 12, Paul is reminding us that transformation happens as our minds are renewed (Rom. 12:2). In other words, as we grow through Bible teaching, we are set free from unhelpful thinking and able to see God's truth. Caring as Jesus cared involves an element of Bible teaching, even if this is just in a small group in a living room, chatting one to one over a coffee, or listening to a sermon online. We might call this 'preventative care' in that it is building us into robust followers of Christ able to navigate life's challenges better because we have God's perspective.

Jesus encouraged even those who were young in the faith to have care and concern for others. The call to 'love one another' and 'care for one another' is not addressed to people who have volunteered to be on a care team or even just those who have a pastoral ministry, part time or full time. It is addressed to us all. And these 'one another' commands include being prepared to 'teach and admonish one another with all wisdom through psalms, hymns, and songs from the Spirit, singing to God with gratitude in your hearts' (Col. 3:16).

Could it be that the reason pastoral care is struggling in many churches is that many Christians are spiritual infants who haven't grown up, or that churches have people who think they are Christians but have never actually come to faith? Hence the mutual care directed by Jesus isn't happening.

Jesus' care means anything is possible

I was once asked to lead a course at a church in the Midlands, on how to set up pastoral care. As I prepared, and thought through the realities of pastoral care, I became enormously discouraged. I recalled times when I felt my own sense of helplessness as a pastor. But this was me looking at things as the Ecclesiastes writer puts it: 'under the sun' (Eccl. 1:14), as opposed to through heaven's eyes. I was forgetting, as we noted earlier, that Jesus healed all who were sick. 'Jesus went throughout Galilee, teaching in their synagogues, proclaiming the good news of the kingdom, and healing every disease and sickness among the people' (Matt. 4:23). 'At sunset, the people brought to Jesus all who had various kinds of illness, and laying his hands on each one, he healed them' (Luke 4:40). This was 'anything is possible' pastoral care!

I remember attending a packed seminar where Johnny Nimmo, a pastor from Germany, was speaking on the value of words of knowledge in evangelism. The subject was not new to me, though I had never had a 'word of knowledge' that had led to a faith sharing opportunity. Towards the end of the seminar, there was opportunity for people to give words of knowledge about other people at the seminar who needed healing. There were around 20 words given, which corresponded to people at the seminar. Johnny then invited anyone who needed healing to come forward and be prayed for by someone who had little experience in praying for healing in that sort of context. So I found myself praying for John, a man in his sixties (I would guess), who had significant hearing loss. I don't actually remember my exact words, but I am guessing that I commanded the ears to get well (in keeping with the seminar's approach and Jesus' own approach to heal with a word of command).

After a few minutes of prayer, John said he felt something significant take place in his ears, which he found hard to describe but resulted in improvement. Later, when Johnny asked for anyone who had been healed to share their story, John spoke of the considerable improvement in hearing that he had enjoyed and gave thanks to me and to God!

I have prayed most of my life but I haven't always expected God to answer immediately – especially in the area of healing. I knew anything was possible but didn't think it was especially likely. I had the opportunity of experiencing first-hand what I had always said I believed, that Jesus' coming changes everything. Anything is possible. For Jesus and the disciples, a follow-up pastoral visit was rarely required. You don't need to return when the problem is resolved!

Granted, if you followed me around as I conducted pastoral visits today, you would see fewer fireworks. But pastoral care in the name of Jesus is to be care that flows from the heart of God. Anything is possible, not because we are trotting out self-help mantras, but because Jesus said if we believed in Him, we would do greater things than Him (John 14:12). The Church has gone on to do all the things Jesus did, and more (though rising from the dead and staying risen is still beyond anyone!).

So what is pastoral care in a church about?
• Pastoral care is expressing love to people in need so that they

may find, deepen, and develop their faith in Jesus.

• Jesus is our chief shepherd who gave His life for His sheep. He cares for us and everyone we seek to care for.

• Jesus is our model who calls us to love the world as He did. We can learn from Him how to live our lives as He did, for the sake of those He calls us to serve.

Questions to consider

• What has been the biblical basis for pastoral care that you have seen practised?

• Are you excited about the idea of ministering like Jesus, or daunted?

• If Jesus attended your pastoral care meetings, what difference would it make?

• Is the Holy Spirit invited to attend your pastoral care meetings?!

03: Understand your role

Conversations about the best violins invariably include talk of the 'Stradivarius', named after the Italian family Stradivari, and particularly Antonio Stradivari who built them during the late seventeenth and early eighteenth century. It is believed that the violins produce a sound like no other, and one instrument today could be worth up to several million US dollars. In 2011, the 'Lady Blunt' violin, dated from 1721 and in pristine condition, was sold in London for $15.9 million. Such is their fame, these ancient instruments have even been scientifically analysed to see if they will reveal the reason for their superior quality. There was clearly a genius to the original design that others have been unable to reproduce or imitate.

God's 'original design' for pastoral care is given in the Bible, and thankfully we don't need scientists to uncover His genius. Jesus is our model for how we should care for others. As we found in chapter 2, pastoral care is expressing love to people in need so that they may find, deepen, and develop their faith in Jesus. In this chapter, we will look at His ongoing role in the life of His Church;

how the early churches structured themselves so that followers of Jesus could lead and manage; and how churches themselves were intended to provide care and nurture. Understanding and identifying with your role, and that of others, is an essential part of ensuring your care improves. However you currently care, you will hopefully understand your care better.

God cares for us

Jesus is the good shepherd and it is evident that this is how the Early Church saw Him. As the risen one, He sent His Spirit (one just like Him) to be our comforter, and reach the parts of our lives that no one else can reach. Paul summed it up well in 2 Corinthians 1:3–7:

> 'Praise be to the God and Father of our Lord Jesus Christ, the Father of compassion and the God of all comfort, who comforts us in all our troubles, so that we can comfort those in any trouble with the comfort we ourselves receive from God. For just as we share abundantly in the sufferings of Christ, so also our comfort abounds through Christ. If we are distressed, it is for your comfort and salvation; if we are comforted, it is for your comfort, which produces in you patient endurance of the same sufferings we suffer. And our hope for you is firm, because we know that just as you share in our sufferings, so also you share in our comfort.'

You will note that God is the comforter 'in all our troubles' and how we receive His comfort is the basis of how we comfort others. Paul does not specify what this may look like, but we can imagine it includes all the ways in which God draws near to us, through His Word, reminding us of what is true of Him and of us, and through the intervening power of the Holy Spirit who gives fresh understanding and relief.

The Holy Spirit is Himself called 'the advocate' in John 14:16, which literally means 'one who comes alongside' and is reference to His work in 'replacing Jesus' who was leaving this earth, but also with respect to His work of strengthening the inner life. Jesus promised the disciples that He would be with them 'to the very end of the age' (Matt. 28:20).

This role of God in caring for His people is vital to grasp and serves us well as we minister, especially when pastoral care means having high doses of empathy and compassion for people. Ultimately though, we need to know that it's not about us and the quality of our care. We cannot fix people. We might like to think we can, but we can't. We are spiritual midwives, assisting what God is doing in giving birth to new life.

God cares through people who lead

The leadership pattern in the Early Church aimed to imitate the servant leadership of Jesus. He was still seen as the 'Chief Shepherd' (1 Pet. 5:4) but human leaders were appointed to oversee and manage a community of believers around the shared life in Christ. Both Peter and Paul taught how leaders were to care for their flock. Paul tells the leaders in Ephesus to 'Keep watch over yourselves and all the flock of which the Holy Spirit has made you overseers. Be shepherds of the church of God, which he bought with his own blood' (Acts 20:28). While Peter writes:

'To the elders among you, I appeal as a fellow elder and a witness of Christ's sufferings who also will share in the glory to be revealed: be shepherds of God's flock that is under your care, watching over them – not because you must, but because you are willing, as God wants you to be; not pursuing dishonest gain, but eager to serve; not lording it over those entrusted to you, but being examples to the flock.' (1 Pet. 5:1–3)

It was clear that shepherding was never to be bullying or controlling but to be aware of what God was doing and to support and encourage it. Their model was the self-giving love of Jesus.

It seems that every church in the New Testament had overseers or elders. (The words seem to be interchangeable for the same role in the church.) These elders served as pastors or shepherds in caring for the church. But there is no assumption that everyone with the gift of pastoring was an elder too.

We too quickly import our twenty-first century notions of leadership and assume that this is how the Church functioned. But Jesus and Paul specifically say that the leadership in the Church is different and avoid the Greek words that imply a certain kind of leadership. Church leadership is not bossing, manipulation, ordering, but guiding, directing, and persuasion. That doesn't mean the leadership was weak. The leaders needed at times to confront and correct any misunderstanding of God's Word, but not from their own egos or agenda. Indeed, Jesus had cautioned them to make sure that they didn't point to themselves:

'But you are not to be called "Rabbi", for you have one Teacher, and you are all brothers. And do not call anyone on earth "father", for you have one Father, and he is in heaven. Nor are you to be called instructors, for you have one Instructor, the Messiah. The greatest among you will be your servant. For those who exalt themselves will be humbled, and those who humble themselves will be exalted.' (Matt. 23:8–12)

But if these leaders had a responsibility to care, a few things were also clear.

No sole pastor

The caring function is shared. As we noted previously, there are no solo pastors in the New Testament; all leadership instructions refer to leaders in plural. The two New Testament characters sometimes thought to be sole pastors (Timothy and Titus) were never addressed as pastors, and are probably apostolic emissaries, sent by Paul to help churches in Ephesus and Crete. Furthermore, they were both charged with the task of appointing elders (plural), not creating a sole pastor model.

We noted in the introduction that one reason many pastors have become 'burnt out' is through not being able to share the pastoral load. Most pastors recognise that this isn't ideal and would appreciate being able to share pastoral care wherever possible while still providing strong leadership.

Pastors equip

The method for how pastors should carry out the Great Commission to 'go and make disciples' (Matt. 28:19) is elaborated by Paul in Ephesians 4:11–13:

> 'So Christ himself gave the apostles, the prophets, the evangelists, the pastors and teachers, to equip his people for works of service, so that the body of Christ may be built up until we all reach unity in the faith and in the knowledge of the Son of God and become mature, attaining to the whole measure of the fullness of Christ.'

There is some scholarly debate over whether 'pastors' and 'teachers' are two separate people or one. An alternative Greek translation could be 'pastors who are also teachers'. Either way, their role is to equip the saints. None of the ministries listed in Ephesians 4 'do' the ministry but rather equip others. The Greek word translated 'equip' is *katartismos*, which is often used as a medical term. In ancient Greece, a doctor would 'equip' a body by resetting a broken bone or relocating a dislocated shoulder.

'Equip' has the idea of bringing something to its full use. In that sense, people represent the raw materials who do not naturally function as intended image bearers of God. Apostles, prophets, evangelists and pastor-teachers are given as gifts and tasked with being the means whereby people – you and me – are better able to serve. All of which dovetails nicely with what we discovered when we looked at Jesus' ministry of care, which has the whole person in mind and is focused on personal transformation.

Pastors are of a particular quality

The epistles of Timothy and Titus give us examples of the kind of qualities the apostle Paul sought, and many have seen these as being the minimum requirement for those who serve:

> 'Here is a trustworthy saying: whoever aspires to be an overseer desires a noble task. Now the overseer is to be above reproach, faithful to his wife, temperate, self-controlled, respectable, hospitable, able to teach, not given to drunkenness, not violent but gentle, not quarrelsome, not a lover of money. He must manage his own family well and see that his children obey him, and he must do so in a manner worthy of full respect. (If anyone does not know how to manage his own family, how can he take care of God's church?) He must not be a recent convert, or he may become conceited and fall under the same judgment as the devil. He must also have a good reputation with outsiders, so that he will not fall into disgrace and into the devil's trap.' (1 Tim. 3:1–7)

'The reason I left you in Crete was that you might put in order what was left unfinished and appoint elders in every town, as I directed you. An elder must be blameless, faithful to his wife, a man whose children believe and are not open to the charge of being wild and disobedient. Since an overseer manages God's household, he must be blameless – not overbearing, not quick-tempered, not given to drunkenness, not violent, not pursuing dishonest gain. Rather, he must be hospitable, one who loves what is good, who is self-controlled, upright, holy and disciplined. He must hold firmly to the trustworthy message as it has been taught, so that he can encourage others by sound doctrine and refute those who oppose it.' (Titus 1:5–9)

These were requirements for overseers or elders in the Early Church that they were looking to appoint, but also key qualities for anyone with a formal role of care within a church today.

To summarise these two passages, the apostle seems to look for three qualities:

i) Character

There is a saying that goes, 'What every church member should be, the church leader has to be.' Though we might not be as strict about the qualities required of someone on a pastoral care team as we are on a leadership team, character is the key quality required. A person involved with pastoral issues really needs to be someone seeking to be an apprentice of Jesus and exhibiting the fruit of that. Of course, they won't be perfect, but there is a difference between 'game-changer' flaws and minor character flaws. We want real people who know the challenge of walking with Christ and who look to His grace.

ii) Commitment

A lot is said about 'being called' to leadership and many, including readers of this book, believe they have received a definite sense from God that they should serve as an elder. However, neither list of attributes includes the words, 'and feels called'. In fact, all Paul says is that 'whoever aspires to be an overseer desires a noble task' (1 Tim. 3:1). It might seem almost too unspiritual for this to be a factor but Paul is basically saying, 'you want people in leadership who want to be there!' Leadership requires commitment to serve and those who want to be there are far more likely to stick to it, no matter the challenges.

iii) Competence

The third quality concerns whether a prospective elder has basic competence to serve. Paul links being able to manage your own household, something many of us do, to competence in managing a church. (Skills such as budgeting finances, planning ahead, taking care of others and managing our time are required in most churches.)

In both passages above, a basic competence to teach God's Word is also listed. Though not every elder is a preacher or teacher, they do need to know the truth well enough to use in personal conversation. Just as Jesus said, 'If you love me, keep my commands' (John 14:15), having a close relationship with God meant applying His Word in congregational life. This was key in the life of the Early Church as it faced doctrinal differences of opinion and heresies for many years.

Many of the following areas of competence would be typical of most people within church life, and their absence would be a concern:

- Knowledge competence – a basic knowledge of the faith, and how humans function (which we will outline in chapter 5) in order to wisely assess both the presenting need and any wider concerns.
- Functional competence – an ability to make arrangements and conduct visits in ways that are helpful, appropriate, keep others informed and have the best interests of the individual at heart.
- Behavioural competence – have a respectful attitude, are wise in maintaining boundaries, discrete and pleasant to be with.
- Ethical competence – a desire to walk with God within the company of His people, maintain relationships and support the values and ethos of their church and its agenda for its people.

Despite the pronoun 'he' in the passages above, these attributes apply to both men and women desirous of being an elder. Marg Mowczko, theologian and blogger, writes:

'Some people think that the qualifications for church leaders recorded in 1 Timothy 3:1–7 and Titus 1:6–9 were written only about men and apply only to men. They believe the implication in these passages is that only men can be church leaders. All of the qualifications listed in 1 Timothy 3:1–7 and Titus 1:6–9, however, can be readily applied to both men and women.

Note that the masculine personal pronouns that appear in many English translations of these passages—and the word "man" that appears in many English translations of verses 1 Timothy 3:1 and Titus 1:6 — are entirely absent in the Greek.

Undoubtedly, most church leaders in early church times were male, and the list of qualifications in 1 Timothy 3:1 assumes an *episkopos* is male, and married, and has children, and has his own household to manage and care for. In fact, *episkopoi* in the early years of the church (circa AD 40–80) were probably relatively wealthy householders who hosted, managed and cared for house churches that met in their own homes. Most householders in the Greco-Roman world were male, but not all. Some householders were women, and some women hosted, managed and cared for house churches (e.g., Lydia and Nympha). Nowhere in the Greek New Testament does it state that church leaders or *episkopoi* must be men.

... The opening sentence of 1 Timothy chapter 3 literally says, "... If someone (or anyone) aspires to 'overseer-ship', s/he desires a fine task." There is no gender preference suggested in this sentence whatsoever.'[1]

There is no doubt that there is a patriarchal influence in the New Testament, but the presence of Phoebe 'a deacon of the church in Cenchreae' (Rom. 16:1) does suggest a trajectory towards men *and* women leading. Women have been church leaders and significant contributors throughout church history, albeit with occasional resistance from their male counterparts.

Some Christians are still divided over this issue, and it may be that you are in a church tradition that believes, or are personally persuaded, that the Bible advocates male leadership. However, what is not debated is that women and men are equally suited to pastoral work.

There are suggestions that some elders or overseers might receive financial support for their work (1 Tim. 5:17–18) based, it would seem, on the Old Testament idea of priests and Levites being supported by the other tribes so that they may serve in the Temple. On occasions, the apostle Paul is supported, and on others, he supports himself.

Ultimately, competent church leaders have the spiritual responsibility for those in their church.

Everyone (potentially) cares

What is abundantly clear in the New Testament is that care is the responsibility of *everyone*.

God has gifted some to be pastors, just as He has given some ministry in evangelism or giving. But every Christian is called to share the faith, give financially – and to care.

It is instructive that the two passages in 1 Timothy and Titus, outlining the qualities for a leader, are the only passages in the New Testament that give the requirements of a leader in such detail. The vast bulk of the material is addressed to everyone. The apostles are keen that we all know and live the truth.

The New Testament regularly encourages all believers to care for one another (John 13:34–35; Gal. 6:2,9–10; Phil. 2:4; 1 Thess. 5:12). Paul's theology is that the Holy Spirit indwells all believers and as they develop His fruit they will naturally care for one another. The gifts of the Spirit 'edifies the church' (1 Cor. 14:4), and edifying others includes caring. Paul is passing on the teaching from Jesus who commanded His disciples to 'love one another' (John 13:35), symbolised by Him washing their feet.

In practice, of course, people are at various stages of their journey in discipleship. Just as you wouldn't put a toddler in charge of the cooking in the kitchen or ask a seven-year-old child to work out the budget, you wouldn't put fragile people in charge of caring for others. They are too in need of care themselves to become who God has made them to be, and this may take considerable time. But even in the early weeks of being a believer, God can still help a new Christian to do something for others.

One helpful way of thinking about pastoral care is to consider care by 'the all', 'the some' and 'the few'[2].

i) 'The all'

We are all exhorted to care for one another. We can all be used to care for others. Much of this is informal, through families, friendship groups and organised small groups.

> 'Let us not lose heart in doing good, for in due time we will reap if we do not grow weary. So then, while we have opportunity, let us do good to all people, and especially to those who are of the household of the faith.' (Gal. 6:9–10, NASB)

Care is exercised as needs are discovered, especially as the Spirit ministers via gifts of encouragement, healing, prophecy, wisdom and knowledge. The assumption of the New Testament is that believers will mature as followers of Christ, know life in Him and be nourished daily by His Word and Spirit.[3]

ii) 'The some'

Certain care may not be suitable by 'the all' because of the time needed or specialism required. In these cases, a select team consisting of people who in their profession (current or past) have expertise, or who have undergone training, and are happy to use their skills for the benefit of the church body, would be more appropriate. Alternatively, mature believers who are followers of Jesus and minister as He did may be 'the some' needed.

iii) 'The few'

These have specialist roles to equip and train the caring ministry of a church. These are sometimes, though not always, those designated 'pastor', 'minister', 'vicar', 'elder' or on staff with a focus on pastoral ministry. They may be what is known as 'lay leaders'.

I suggested earlier that the New Testament does not encourage sole pastors, however, in some settings, it may be practically impossible to have more than one pastor. The church may be full of young believers not able to take a leadership role, or the culture may assume the pastor or vicar takes a lead, and it can take time for the sole pastor to educate the church towards a body ministry. But these are exceptions; it's wise and biblical for any full-time staff to share pastoral care needs with others, whether also full-time, part-time or volunteer.

What about you?

Consideration of the role according to the Bible may help your understanding of what you are doing.

If you are an elder, overseer or in a pastoral role, your work is to serve church members so that they are nurtured and built up in the faith. It is an essentially equipping role, so that the people become able to live as Jesus lived, and care for one another. Remember, Jesus is their shepherd and the Holy Spirit their guide, not you. You are like a fellow employee seeking to discern what the boss is looking to do and reminding them about company policy in certain respects! Any advice you give is in the light of how Jesus may be guiding them.

You may know that within the history of the Church, some pastoral carers have assumed that they were responsible for the holiness of the congregation and created a culture of fear akin to an ultra-strict boarding school. Your role doesn't give you a right to be nosey and judgmental. God is at work in the people you serve, so you are looking to see what He is doing and could be doing. You are an overseer not an inquisitor! And if you are a woman, who thought you were barred from leadership because of gender, but who has all the other qualities required of an elder, maybe it's time to think again.

Let's be clear that whoever you are, if you are part of the body of Christ, you can care for those around you. You don't need a special role for that. You have gifts, which the Spirit wants you to use in His service, as opportunity arises and as time allows. If you have a family, that will be the best place to start.

Questions to consider

• How comfortable are you in your pastoral role, if you have one?

_____

_____

• Are you happy caring for others even if you don't have a formal pastoral role?

_____

_____

• If you are in a full-time role, how can you share opportunities with others? Are you willing to delegates, even if you fear their care may not be (at least initially) as good as you may like?

_____

_____

[1]Marg Mowczko, 'Paul's qualifications for church leaders (1 Timothy 3)', posted 5 August 2010, taken from margmowczko.com [Accessed March 2019]
[2]These headings are taken from 'ACC – Framework for Good Practice in Pastoral Care', taken from acc-org.uk [Accessed March 2019]
[3]The Paraclesis course, available at CWR, aims to help Christians recognise how God helps them on their journey and, in turn, become able to assist others on theirs. This encourages a more mentoring style of help, where those going through an issue are matched with people who have come through the same issue, eg major health challenge, divorce, unemployment, childlessness, bereavement. (Visit paraclesis.org.uk)

Part 2

Essential practice

04: Create a culture of care

While working as a Christian student worker, I took a group of students to help an independent evangelical church in Canterbury with their local outreach. They were hoping to plant a church in a disused Anglican church and needed a team to do some door-to-door work to gauge the interest of the local community.

Prior to this trip I had asked the pastor, Gordon Dalzell, about his philosophy of pastoral ministry, and he shared the journey he had been on. At one point, he said, 'It was then I realised that you can't have elders if you don't have a church!'

'Excuse me?' I looked at him puzzled.

'It came to me as I was sitting in a large church, and the talk was about how we should love one another. I realised that in a church of this size, the command was rather hard to practise. Like many churches, it was just a gathering of believers: people who attend a regular worship service in the same building, singing the same songs and hearing the same sermons. But the injunctions in the New Testament to love one another are completely lost on them because they don't know one another closely enough to know what love would look like.'

'And how does eldership fit in?'

Gordon continued: 'The New Testament elder functioned as someone who was to teach and live out the faith, as an example to the believers. The fellow believers can only benefit from that if they know him and he them. Hence, many churches today are not really churches, and so consequently it's impossible for them to be led by elders in any meaningful sense.'

It was this conversation that began my serious reflections on pastoral life and the development of a culture of care. Gordon was alluding to what is sometimes known as 'body life', which highlights the New Testament metaphor of the Church as a body, where the interconnectedness of the believers provides strength and sustenance, and a context for care to take place.

We saw in the last chapter that care is provided by those who oversee the church (labels vary depending on the denomination or church stream). In addition, it is clear that everyone can potentially be involved, and some may want to be part of a team of people who have the time and gifting to assist in the work. But we have also noted that care is much broader than the alleviation of pain. Anyone we care for can be seen as part of God's ongoing purposes towards maturity as a believer in Jesus. If this culture is not generated, the church leaders will be caught up in an increasing frenzy of care, and it will be hard for the church and its members to grow.

In this chapter, we will be focusing on how we can create a culture where people care for one another.

Culture shift?

Acknowledging that pastoral care is a church-wide activity and involves us all in becoming apprentices to Jesus requires a culture shift in many churches. Typically, many churches are measured on the indices of A, B and C: Attendance, Buildings and Cash. How many come? Is the building suitable? Can we pay our bills? If each of these is positive, the church leaders feel buoyant.

These are not unimportant matters, but there are two further indices to consider, D and E: Discipleship and Evangelism. How many of those who come are intentionally apprentices of Jesus? How well are we sharing the good news of the kingdom with those who haven't yet responded? Or to put it another way: are we expressing love to those in need that they may find, deepen and develop a faith in Jesus?

If things are not going so well in a church, leaders can understandably feel a bit defeated and may find factors in their local situation for why God doesn't seem to be working as powerfully in their church compared to others. And they might be right in thinking that. But by continuing to trust God, leaders can rejoice for other churches where amazing things are happening and aim to retain a more triumphant mindset of 'it could happen here!' If churches see people become Christians, it must be possible in any church. If churches are seeing people become disciples, it must be possible where we are. If churches see people healed, it must be possible where we are. You get the idea. Anytime anyone says, 'Well, that won't happen here', maybe respond by asking, 'Why not?'

What is 'church culture'?

Sam Chand says, 'culture is the strongest force in any organization. The best way to understand culture is the statement: "This is how we do things here.".... It is the atmosphere in which the church functions. It is the prevalent attitude. It is the collage of spoken and unspoken messages.'[1]

If we want to establish a culture that values and practises pastoral care within the body, as the New Testament encourages, we first need to look at the present culture.

As first-century men, the disciples were used to the rabbinic model of imitating the Rabbi, and so had responded positively to the invitation to 'follow me', but were slow to realise that this was a call to deny themselves and take up their cross daily. Today, we might also forget the implications of being a follower of Christ.

People will attend church for all manner of reasons:

• I attend because my family do and I want to be compliant.
• I attend because I have a vague idea that it is good for me.
• I attend because that's what God wants and life will go better as a result.
• I attend when I can amidst other appealing activities.
• I attend because it's part of being an apprentice of Jesus. I look to learn how to do that better and make contributions where I can.
• I attend and bring friends and family along to introduce them to the faith.

Whatever their reasons for attending, over time, people will sense culture of a church. They may feel challenged. They may feel uncomfortable. They may be intrigued. They may be repelled. They may feel all of these in the same service...

A new culture is established in a number of ways.

Mission and vision statements

If you randomly google well-known local churches, you will invariably find the phrase 'spiritual growth' on their website and ways that church aims to create means whereby people actually grow spiritually. Unfortunately, not every church is able to fulfil the lofty ambitions of the discipleship element of their mission statements but ideally church leaders need to look for ways for its people to grow as followers of Christ.

The terms 'mission' and 'vision' are often used interchangeably. 'Vision' is typically the broad aim of where you are heading, and 'mission', how you are going to get there. But sometimes they are used in a directly opposite fashion!

Here's a few examples of mission and vision statements:

- 'To be a Christ-centred church in an influential city, which multiplies and helps other churches towards these shared goals, across the region, western Europe and beyond.'
- 'Together as a church family we are striving to love God, the community, and each other, through worship, learning, service, caring and mission.'
- 'We seek to be friendly and contemporary in styles of worship and teaching. We seek to relate the Bible to daily life and develop warm relationships within the church family and the wider community.'
- 'Save, equip, and send out a highly motivated army of believers who engage every segment of society while remaining true to our DNA.'
- 'To win people to Jesus Christ, train believers to become disciples, and send disciples out to impact the world.'

• 'To spread the gospel in our community by reaching out in love and respect to people from every nation.'

If your church has no vision statement, why not develop one? Get the leaders, or a group of interested folk, together and discuss what your vision is in the light of the biblical mandate to make and equip disciples. Developing a vision statement will not in itself establish a church culture, but it will help those involved to think about direction and how to channel time and resources in the direction of that vision. If your vision is compelling for those in the engine room of the church, others are sure to catch the enthusiasm.

The teaching

As church members, we need to be reminded through teaching that the good news of Jesus includes the discipleship invitation, and the implications of this for expressing love to those in need.

In coming to faith, God imparts His Spirit to us, which provides a new power to live. Many themes will be covered within the teaching of any church, of course, but the wider context is that, along with all the New Testament churches, Christians are learning to put to death inbuilt tendencies against God's way, and embrace this new life within them.

In many churches, the assumption is that having responded to Jesus, we are 'in' – and there is no real expectation of growth, or any honesty about the weekly struggles to live for Christ where He has placed us. So it is essential that a church's teaching curriculum reflects the need to equip the church. If Jesus was concerned to help His disciples grow, the local expression of His body needs to be focused on the same thing.

The worship

There's no doubt that the songs and style of music contributes to the culture of a church for good or ill. Whatever your personal preference (ancient, modern, or ancient and modern), what happens in sung worship corporately sets the tone for much that follows.

I had the opportunity to interview on radio Lee Kricher, pastor of Amplify Church in Pittsburgh. In his book, *Reaching the Next Generation*[2], he said that it's unlikely that younger adults will be drawn to a service where the people in visible leadership are significantly older than they are. So his church has instituted a rule requiring that 75% of worship leaders in visible roles be 35 years old or younger, since that's the average age of the community they seek to serve. The church had nosedived numerically and is now pushing several thousand again.

Other communities may have a more mixed demographic but it is helpful to reflect whether aspects of corporate worship could be more varied in style and whether those in leadership could be more sensitive to the needs of all as the church moves to a more inclusive culture of care.

Specific focus on equipping care

Teaching and worship can equip the congregation, but, ideally, there needs to be a number of options for this to happen further. Sunday services are often doing many different things including helping outsiders grasp what the Christian faith is about. Often, there is too little time on Sundays to tease out how the Word applies to daily life, and not in a specific way required by people at various stages of faith development. Instead a church will use mid-week small groups for this kind of thing, preparing them for all that life throws at them. Small groups, short courses, mentoring, coaching and counselling can be better tools to ensure that the implications of discipleship are unpacked for individuals.

I call this 'equipping care' because it is helping to develop a person's life with God, and a resilience to weather the various challenges that could tip them over into a crisis where they fail to function well and need intervention from someone on the pastoral team. At the simplest level, someone who has come to faith believing that all will be smooth now that God is involved may suffer a faith crisis when their prayers are not answered as they hoped and life becomes seemingly trickier than before they came to faith. Wise and sensible Bible teaching can help measure their expectations. There are a multitude of ways in which the default settings of our minds have been created by the world's outlook and not that given by God, and Bible teaching can help us reframe our outlook.

Scottish pastor William Still said: 'My pastoral work of personal dealing, considerable though it is, has been greatly reduced through the years because the building up of men's faith by the Word of God solves so much in their lives... that instead of becoming a liability on my time and energy, they become pastors themselves.'[3]

Or we can go five centuries further back to the great reformer, Martin Luther, who said: 'No man is to be alone against Satan; God instituted the church and the ministry of the Word in order that we might join and help one another. If the prayer of one does not help, the prayer of the other will.'[4]

Ultimately, it is God's Spirit who creates the culture. We play our part in putting ourselves in the way of the Spirit through prayer, Bible study, meeting with God's people and other means that are open to God's people. But it is He who changes hearts.

But calling this 'equipping care' is not in any way suggesting that we become self-sufficient, or that good Bible teaching and equipping means we won't need reactive care when blindsided by a crisis, illness or tragedy. It does mean that we must not underplay and undervalue the way in which church life and appropriate teaching helps to nurture and prepare people.

It was missionary surgeon Denis Parsons Burkitt who famously remarked: 'If people are constantly falling off a cliff, you could place ambulances under the cliff or build a fence on the top of the cliff. We are placing all too many ambulances under the cliff.'[5]

If we are caring for others but never working with them to assist them in any underlying issues that are creating the problems then we are failing to make apprentices of Jesus, ensuring that sooner or later they will 'fall off a cliff'.

Too often couples come for counselling already damaged by words and activity that create wounds from which recovery is slow. Courses on marriage for engaged and married couples help people establish stable marriages. Children grow up lacking the nurture they need to establish healthy attachments. Courses on parenting help parents better manage their children. Courses on finance help people manage income and outgoings so that debt is not an issue. Courses are not a cure-all, but they are a start.

Places for care

Thus far we have noted the value of creating an educational environment to help people's lives, but this does not in and of itself create the kind of body life whereby people open up to others about what is going on. When someone has a physical need, it becomes obvious to everyone that care is required. But so many needs do not have an obvious outward manifestation and as such people can live with the need, unsure of how to express it, or unwilling to do so. Physical needs in most churches function a little like the visible part of an iceberg. They represent only 10% while 90% of the need is never seen or acknowledged, such as emotional pain, spiritual need, mental health or relational concerns.

Thus, it is wise for churches to create opportunities for people to mix around shared activities. This is valuable anyway, but also gives space for needs to surface, and help given that they may enjoy the abundant life Jesus offers. Adults are, of course, quite capable of organising themselves but with a little work, it's not difficult to create opportunities, if only on a semi-regular basis. I have known churches that have run sports clubs (football, cricket etc) rambling groups (some call that a sport...), knitting, crochet, board games, Scalextric, model railway, cooking, eating desserts (yes I know...), chess, watching films, reading books, singing (of course).

If you were signing up to be on a pastoral care team you might not have this kind of thing in mind, but as people gather and do stuff, conversations start and needs are uncovered and expressed. In most cases, attending, chatting and maybe praying are sufficiently therapeutic; in others, where it's clear that some other kind of intervention is required, a person may be referred on to more specialist pastoral care.

Reactive care

Most churches develop teams of people who have the time, are gifted and able to react to meet pastoral care needs.

We know that although everyone *can* be involved in care, not everyone *does*. We know that those appointed as pastors cannot, and should not, do it all, for the sake of their own health and sanity. The pastoral care team is made up of full-timers, part-timers and volunteers to serve the needs of the church and those in the orbit of the church. In some cases, they cover the needs of those not included in the existing networks, particularly small groups. In other cases, they provide care that the networks are not equipped to provide because of the longevity or the complexity of the need.

Reactive care is required in situations such as illness, bereavement, hospitalisation, unemployment, loss of faith, debt, addiction and relational breakdown (marriage, family, church family). We will consider how we engage in this kind of care in a later chapter.

The follow through

Ultimately in life, we can determine our priorities by what we make time for and give attention to.

Church culture is set by what we permit and deny in our services and in the weekly activities of the church. It's unlikely that any of the churches activities have no value, but are they taking up time and attention that could be best focused upon equipping pastoral care? What is happening mid-week in the course of a year that is equipping God's people for works of service, including pastoral care training?

Many church leaders find that establishing this kind of culture from scratch takes a long time, but there are typically some people who 'get it' early on in whom the leaders can invest time and training. It may require less energy being put elsewhere in order that building a healthy culture receives prime attention. Not everyone welcomes change and sometimes, as a instigator of change, you might feel like you are a lone ranger but don't despair.

God lives by His Spirit in His people and they are longing to be more like Jesus – they just don't know it yet! You can pray. You can ask good questions. You can gently point out needs.

Bob works as a software engineer and meets with two other guys as a prayer triplet; Carla is a newly married wife of a non-believing husband who gets together for coffee with a group of women each week; Doug helps out with the homeless project and catches up with the leader, Tim.

Just a snapshot of people in a church. Each has regular interactions that are sometimes superficial, sometimes serious as they grapple with faith and life in the twenty-first century. None of them would be on a 'pastoral care list', but each may need some mature counsel from time to time.

But there will be those who require an appointment with a carer. Once a culture of caring and discipling are established, it is much easier for any carer to have a deeper conversation with someone about how they are relating to God in and through what they are facing. They might quote something preached recently, or a study considered. It is a tough ask to launch into deeper 'walking and growing with Christ' issues in a church where the only discipleship sermon was eight months ago. But if such talk is part of the church, it's much easier.

Would you feel comfortable walking up to someone and discussing body fat percentages? Probably not. But if you are in weight loss class and measuring body fat was the topic of the last gathering, suddenly the more intrusive comments about body fat is regarded as a normal conversation.

Similarly, if you are talking about living God's Word and the challenges that temptations bring, it is much easier to broach these kind of topics, for mutual benefit, in a visit. And if this was the mutual expectation within church, then, naturally, we would talk about personal growth.

I interviewed Bruce Collins about his time as vicar of Christchurch Kenton, a church he transitioned from being standard evangelical to charismatic. He said that there were four groups of people to bear in mind when initiating a change in culture:

The radicals – you make a hole in the wall and the radicals are happy to run through it, no questions asked.

The progressives – they look at the hole in the wall and are initially unsure that you really needed to make the hole but will think it through and eventually come round. They may well be parents of the radicals.

The conservatives – they are aghast that it was necessary to make a hole and even after hearing the explanation are uncertain that it should ever be done.

The traditionalists – these people have an emotional attachment to the way things used to be and are never going to like holes of any kind anywhere! But, providing their needs are met, they are happy for holes to be made and, if they are comfortable, may even be happy to fund them.

As a church establishes a culture of care, it might take a while for some people to get on board and some never will – but the church belongs to Jesus, so do it anyway!

Questions to consider

- Does your church have a vision statement?
- If you had to form a vision around what is happening now in your church, would that be something you would feel positive about?

_____

_____

- If people came into your church, what culture would they pick up?

_____

_____

- Do particular congregations have their own special cultures?

_____

_____

- Would you say your church has a culture of care? If so, how did it develop? If not, why not?

_____

_____

[1]Samuel R. Chand, _Cracking Your Church's Culture_ (Hoboken, NJ, USA: Jossey-Bass, 2010)
[2]Lee Kricher, _Reaching the Next Generation_ (Grand Rapids, MI, USA: Zondervan, 2016)
[3]William Still, _Word of the Pastor_ (Tain, Scotland: Christian Focus Publications, 2011)
[4]Martin Luther, _Luther's Works_, Vol 54 (Minneapolis, MN, USA: Augsburg Fortress, 1959) p78
[5]D. P. Burkitt, H. C. Trowell _Western diseases, their emergence and prevention_ (Cambridge: Harvard University Press, 1981)

05: Understand how people typically function

We have seen that pastoral care is expressing love to people in need, and that these needs will include their relationship with God in addition to physical needs, which are the classic concerns of pastoral care. But we are in danger of over-simplification if we presume that people's needs simply fall into the body or soul category. Indeed, this is not how Jesus saw people, even though He was concerned for people's bodies and souls and healed both.

We get an insight into how Jesus sees people in His response to a question.

'One of the teachers of the law came and heard them debating. Noticing that Jesus had given them a good answer, he asked him, "Of all the commandments, which is the most important?"

"The most important one," answered Jesus, "is this: 'Hear, O Israel: The Lord our God, the Lord is one. Love the Lord your God with all your heart and with all your soul and with all your mind and with all your strength.' The second is this: 'Love your neighbour as yourself.'

There is no commandment greater than these."' (Mark 12:28–31)

Jesus' response is based on His Father's commands in Deuteronomy 6:4–7 where we read we have different parts of us, which are to be offered to God in love and worship: the heart, mind, soul and strength. In the midst of figuring out what may be wrong with someone we care for, we are wise to have some kind of grid for how people typically function.

Selwyn Hughes, the founder of CWR, developed an approach based on his understanding of Scripture and how Jesus saw people.[1] Selwyn's approach will form the basis of this chapter.

A biblical understanding of the human personality

An understanding of who we are begins with God. God's personality has the following qualities: He is spiritual (Gen. 1:1–2), rational (Isa. 55:8), volitional (Isa. 43:18–19), emotional (Gen. 6:5–6) and physical (Gen. 2:7). Selwyn believed that because we are made 'in God's image', these five characteristics of God are likely to constitute our image.

We are:
• Spiritual or longing beings
• Rational or thinking beings
• Volitional or choosing beings
• Emotional or feeling beings
• Physical beings

Selwyn was not alone in his thinking. A.W. Tozer wrote, 'God is a person, and in the deep of His mighty nature He thinks, wills, enjoys, feels, loves, desires and suffers as any other person may.'[2]

Sadly, our understanding of humanity has to include the fact that we became 'sinful' beings. We inherit the sin virus passed down to us from our divine forefathers, Adam and Eve. Although they were dwelling with God in Eden, they succumbed to the temptation from Satan to believe lies about God and in their disobedience suffered the punishment that God had warned them about. They were estranged from God and each other, and would one day suffer physical death.

Selwyn explained that we are both dignified and fallen. The image of God has been defaced by sin but it is still within us though broken, disfigured and fragmented (Gen. 9:6). The consequences of the Fall can be observed in the attitudes and actions of people, which are damaging, degrading and even, in some situations, depraved.

Selwyn believed that deep within every person is a powerful motivation to know:

• Security (unconditional love)
• Self-worth (value)
• Significance (meaning)

We cannot function in the way that we were designed unless our needs are met by God, so these crucial needs become powerful motivators.

As James K.A. Smith said:

'To be human is to be for something, directed toward something, oriented toward something. To be human is to be on the move, pursuing something, after something. We are like existential sharks: we have to move to live. We are not just static containers for ideas; we are dynamic creatures directed toward some end. In philosophy we have a shorthand term for this: something that is oriented toward an end or telos (a "goal") is described as "teleological." Augustine rightly recognizes that human beings are teleological creatures.'[3]

At heart, our behaviour comes from our motivation, even if that motivation is sometimes not clear to us. We may even have conflicting motivations, which make decisions especially hard; for example, I want to be a successful at my job and also available for my children; I want to say the hard things God is calling me to say, and be popular.

Selwyn Hughes' approach to counselling, known as 'The Waverley Model' (now the Waverley Integrative Framework), develops the idea that being aware of the five areas of human functioning, mentioned above, may be a factor in helping people navigate whatever need has come their way. We will briefly look at each of these five elements.

We are spiritual beings

God designed us to have our needs met in Him, in His Word and within loving relationships with others. The deep longings that are totally satisfied in God are partly assuaged by alternatives. We might believe that money will be the answer to life's problems, or dabble in various drugs. We might pursue fame, believing that making a name for ourselves will tick our emotional boxes. These alternatives may soothe us for a while but it's like we are thirsty and need pure mountain water but are making do with polluted rain water instead. It only gives temporary satisfaction.

Our core problem is idolatry: putting something or someone in the place that God alone should have in our lives. Throughout the Bible, we saw how God demonstrated His commitment to humanity only for people to trust in other sources instead. As Saint Augustine famously put it: 'God has made us for Himself and our hearts are restless 'til they find their rest in him.'[4]

As we reflect on our own inadequacies in caring, we are wise to be aware that everyone's longings ultimately need to be focused on God. Our security, self-worth and significance are found in Him. In our care for others, we are wise not to collude in idolatry. There are people and things that can replace God; for example, if only I was married, if only I had stayed single, if only I had children, if only my children behaved well, if only we had our own house, if only I had a better job, if only I had more time to...

These may be legitimate longings but if they are deemed 'the' solution, they are dangerously close to being idolatrous and will not result in finding peace. While not forgetting a person's chief need, part of pastoral care is to encourage people to look to God, to seek Him, to cast all anxiety on Him (1 Pet. 5:7).

We are thinking beings

It was wrong thinking that led to the Fall in the Garden of Eden. The serpent injected doubts about the goodness and reliability of God, and Adam and Eve fell for them, disobeying God's Word.

What we think about is intrinsic to being human. The Bible talks of the way in which our foolish minds were darkened before we came to faith. However, it was a positive thought that then enabled us to join God's kingdom. We heard or read about God's love and the good news of the gospel and received it as truth. It may have taken a time of questioning and reflection, but eventually we had it clear enough in our minds to take action.

Question: What are thoughts?

Answer: Our thoughts are the ways in which we are conscious of things, and are linked closely to our beliefs and our memories.

The three 'I's in thinking:

• Ideas: the main things you are thinking about.

- Information: what is true about life.
- Images: mental pictures of life (some reflecting the information we have received, others a construct we have put on the information, which may not have anything to do with reality).

Many Christians want their thinking to be transformed so that it is more and more based on God's truth and less and less on the lies they receive daily from the media and those around them: lies about where true value is found, what life is, and how to be a success in life.

One corrected idea can make a massive difference. For example, someone might see God as a judge and be very careful to always do the right thing. They might then hear that God loves them, He likes them and that He is easy to be with. Relating to a loving God might take some getting used to for that person but might also make a big transformation in their thinking.

In pastoral care, it's good to pay attention to the fruits of people's thinking. We won't know for sure all that they are thinking, but we can ascertain what may be going on by what they say, and how they answer questions. We are aware that the imagination can play a big part in assessing life, and that memories of past events often influence a person's thinking when faced with an event or problem that they might have faced before; for example, a person might react badly to criticism because it reminds them of a parent whose constant criticism made them nervous. We can help them think well in the way we handle the situation and suggest approaches based on wisdom and knowledge of God's Word.

We are feeling beings

It has been well said that feelings are great servants but lousy masters. Our modern age lives by the slogan, 'If it feels good, do it'. We often ask people how they feel, not how they think. We talk of hurting someone's feelings more than harming someone's thinking. Feelings can all too easily govern our lives.

But feelings are deceptive: they can make us do things that we know are not correct, and they can change so fast that we don't know where we are and what we 'feel'. If how we lived was based solely on how we felt, we would get into a lot of trouble! And of course many do. In films, books and TV programmes, feelings are what make the characters interesting, 'real', move our emotions, create tension, make us care and keep us engaged. But many people believe that they *have* to live according to how they feel. They believe it would be unbearable if their feelings were not satisfied.

By and large, we can change feelings by changing our thinking; we can't change thinking by changing feelings. We have all had times when feelings probably played a large role as our inner world was formed. Feelings such as anger, fear and lust spread; habitual patterns of bitterness and depressive moods can overtake our whole life and become the fabric of who we are and how we operate. Feelings are often too complex and powerful for us to simply will change by our own willpower; our minds need to be renewed.

Transformation

Jesus wants us to tune into our feelings, so that they are part of the positive transformation of character (Gal. 5:16–26). It is not a simple matter of telling them to 'get in line'. We can think and choose courses of action, which will help us resolve negative feelings. We can learn to handle unpleasant feelings with wisdom, knowing what to do and how to respond – not repressing or denying our feelings, but allowing them to lead us to trust and to be further involved with God.

The ABC theory of emotion

An interesting formula for understanding how thinking affects our feelings was devised by Albert Ellis[5]. It is called the 'ABC theory of emotion', and was used by Selwyn Hughes in his teaching.

A – Activating experience

B – Beliefs (the perception of the event and our thoughts concerning the event)

C – Consequent emotions (and resulting thoughts / behaviour), which may be addressed by:

D – Disputing irrational ideas (thoughts / behaviour)

E – New emotional consequence or effect

Ellis suggested that an activating experience (A) does not control the consequent emotions (C) directly – it has got to go through a person's beliefs (B). So an event is emotionally neutral, but our emotions and feelings depend upon our beliefs about that event. To see transformation take place in our lives, we must make sure that our beliefs accord with God's Word, not with the worldly thinking we have picked up. God's Word enables us to dispute wrong ideas (D) leading to a new effect (E).

It can be easy to oversimplify at this point but feelings will start to change as we think correctly about our life in God; as we recognise those feelings that are destructive and seek to cultivate ones that are in keeping with the heart of God.

We need to be very discerning when handling our feelings. They are like warning lights on a car's dashboard showing that something is wrong. In some cases, feelings may be a symptom of something that has nothing to do with the inner life – tiredness, hunger or physical pain – while in others, specialist help from a trained counsellor may be needed.

In caring for people, it is valuable to observe the person and listen to the emotions. We needn't assume that how they are with us is standard. They may be 'pulling themselves together' in our presence. We need to validate how they are feeling and, as appropriate, sympathise or suggest further counselling. As we speak truth and hope and inject some helpful approaches, with God's help we can help others to find resolution and hope.

We are choosing beings

It is only after considering our thoughts and our feelings that we come to our heart. This dimension of the self is known by various words: heart describes the location; will describes its behaviour; and spirit, in that its nature is spiritual. Whatever we call it, it's the place where the choosing happens!

The heart operates like a CEO within the self. We are defined by the choices we make: our consents and non-consents, which form the character – 'I will not do this, I will do that.' We become known as someone who habitually sings, or rages, or swears, or laughs. Those behaviours flow from a steady series of decisions we make, which lead to developing a particular character.

Some preachers and sport coaches focus on wrong behaviour: 'Stop doing that – it's wrong. Do this instead!' This may result in the outcome they want, but if they start there they are heading for problems later on because they fail to deal with the mind, which needs transformation. Someone may 'do' different things on the basis of advice from an advisor, but never really changes from within, because his or her thoughts and feelings remain unchanged.

Your capacity to choose God and follow Jesus will be a result of how you think about Him, what you know He wants of you, how you feel about that and whether your body is in line to function appropriately. But, of course, the will also has a place within your internal loop.

The choosing sequence:
what we think + how we feel = what we do

As you grow in awareness of your thoughts, feelings and how to manage your body, you are more able to consciously choose to follow Jesus. If your spare time is spent watching 18-rated films, listening to music with unhelpful lyrics, reading horror fiction and never reading Scripture, you will not know what Jesus calls you to do, least of all do it. It is sobering to note that many make little progress in their Christian life because they don't want to! They know they should want to, they know it makes sense but when they read about Jesus and His teaching, they prefer life as it is.

Wants can be obvious: 'I want to be married'; not so obvious: 'I can't decide what job I want'; or even conflicting: 'I want to have a life, but I also have an obligation to my elderly mother whom I want to be happy.'

Jesus wants you to get to the point where your will is so close to His – but that won't happen overnight. There are four steps required:

1. Desire to be willing.
2. Surrender to God's will.
3. Be content with God's will.
4. Participate in God's will.

The apostle Paul could say of himself:

'I have been crucified with Christ and I no longer live, but Christ lives in me. The life I now live in the body, I live by faith in the Son of God, who loved me and gave himself for me.' (Gal. 2:20)

In practice, our heart often wavers in its commitments to situations, people and causes. Sometimes we delude ourselves that we are 'fully committed' when our behaviour says otherwise. In caring for others, we look at the choices they have taken and are making. We know that they will be governed by how they think (what they know) and how they feel. We will want them to make wise choices, to be clear about what they want and how this ties in with their faith.

We are physical beings

Jesus said that we should love the Lord with all our strength, yet the body is often overlooked when it comes to personal development. By 'body' we mean the physical side of life through which the other dimensions of the self (the mind, heart and soul) operate.

We are whole people, and our bodies often reflect the inner self. This means that we can often spot what is going on in the inside from the outside: our personality shines through our body. The body is the place from which we interact with our environment. Through the body, we touch, taste, see, hear and smell the world around us. We come to God as people in bodies, as God planned, and although our body can overwhelm us with its impulses, it is intended by God to be the place where God Himself dwells.

Jesus had the same type of human body on earth as we do today, and He used it to fulfil the Father's purpose. He was not subject to His body, but rather made the body the place of blessing for the world.

Often our choices and intentions can follow the impulses of the body, and thus throw God's purpose for us into disarray. Alternatively, the body can follow our decisions. We have the same choice before us as Adam and Eve in the Garden of Eden: unhelpful human desires or obedience to God. With the help of the Holy Spirit, we can reject the human impulses that take us away from God and submit our bodies by conscious decision to God. This is what Paul means in Romans 12:1 when he calls on Christians to 'offer [their] bodies as a living sacrifice'. Our bodies are part of an internal feedback loop, which operates as regularly as a machine. Indeed in extreme forms, such as addictions, people will say that they cannot help their behaviour. The truth is that more people are addicted to bodily actions than we realise – hence those words of Jesus: 'the spirit is willing, but the body is weak!' (Matt. 26:41, NLT).

Before we came to faith, we consciously or unconsciously developed habits; if you place self at the centre of your life, then your body will want to gratify itself. For example, in Philippians 3:19 when Paul is talking about those who live as enemies of the cross of Christ, he says: 'Their destiny is destruction, their god is their stomach'.

GOD'S ORDER	HUMAN ORDER
GOD	BODY
SPIRIT	HEART
SOUL	MIND
MIND (thinking and feeling)	SPIRIT
HEART	SOUL
BODY	GOD

We may have a new life in Jesus but still operate according to our old life, as if using an old programme. But as the Word of God and the Spirit of God do their work, we embrace a new life. Generally, care is given when the body is not functioning well. It may be appropriate to invite God to heal what's not working and His grace for whatever is being faced.

Soul

The soul is sometimes used synonymously with 'spiritual' and is perhaps the most complex part of the self to describe, partly because it is hidden within the depths of the self.

> 'The soul is that aspect of your whole being that correlates, integrates and enlivens everything going on in the various dimensions of the self. It regulates whatever is occurring in each dimension and how it interacts with the others. The soul is 'deep' in the sense of being foundational and also in the sense that it lies almost totally beyond conscious awareness.'[6]

Christians differ in what they believe constitutes the soul. Some include the mind, will and emotions within the soul. The soul has been described as functioning in our life like the hard drive in the computer, which works in the background as our life carries on. Or perhaps like the central heating system in a large office, which keeps the temperature pleasant and is only noticed when it goes wrong. Most people barely know and recognise the soul, not least because some have concluded that it doesn't exist, but it is a vital part of who we are. It is spiritual in nature and as Dallas Willard explains, it serves to link the parts of the self together. When God acts to liberate the spirit, the soul too is brought alive to God.

Caring for the whole person

Although this chapter is not intended to be a substitute for proper training in counselling, I hope it gives you areas to look for. The person may be presenting one need but it actually may be a symptom of others, or is not as major as others. As you look through God-shaped spectacles, you can at least have a good idea of what may be going on, prayerfully seek to work with God in what He is looking to do and express love to people in need. Helping people to find, develop and deepen their faith in Jesus is caring for them in the way He would. It's a wise approach for us all to take on board.

Questions to consider

• Do you have a framework in mind when you talk with people who you are seeking to care for?

• How comfortable are you thinking about the broader elements of the human personality?

• Do you know a counsellor who you could refer people to?

[1] A detailed outline of the approach can be found in the book *Christ Empowered Living* by Selwyn Hughes (Farnham: CWR, 2005) or *Care and Counselling* by Ron Kallmier (Farnham: CWR, 2011)

[2] A.W. Tozer, *The Pursuit of God: The Human Thirst for the Divine* (Camp Hill, PA, USA: Christian Publications, 1993)

[3] James K.A. Smith, *You Are What You Love: The Spiritual Power of Habit* (Ada, MI, USA: Brazos Press, 2016)

[4] *The Confessions of Saint Augustine*, translated by Rex Warner (New York, USA: Mentor, 1963)

[5] A. Ellis, 'Rational Psychotherapy and Individual Psychology', *Journal of Individual Psychology*, Vol 13, 1957) pp38–44

[6] Dallas Willard and Don Simpson, *Revolution of Character* (Colorado Springs, CO, USA: Navpress, 2005)

06: Adopt a biblical approach to suffering

A question that always ranks highly in objections to the Christian faith is framed something like this: 'If there is a God of love, why does He allow suffering?'

It's rarely a purely academic question. Often the person asking has known particular suffering themselves or been pained by the suffering of others. What seems to be a philosophical question is a very real one for them. Personal suffering is the reason that some people give for leaving the faith. The implicit message is: 'This is not what I signed up for. I thought God would prevent this from happening. Maybe I don't believe after all.' At some point, perhaps you have asked the very same question yourself.

Here's some of the crises people face:

• Bereavement through death of a close relative or friend
• Onset of physical disability
• Chronic long-term illness
• Termination of employment
• Children leaving home

• A reduced sense of independence through age or illness
• A perceived reduction of status on ceasing a significant role
• Ageing – reduction in capacity and choices
• A significant reduction in finances or possessions (car / home)
• Bankruptcy
• Retirement from employment
• Marriage breakdown
• The end of long-term supportive relationships
• Sense of alienation from God
• The surrender of life goals because they appear unreachable
• Loss of childhood through deprivation, abuse, family breakdown

As you care for people, you might be asked about pain and
suffering. How might you respond?

Some general points:

• Remember the adage, 'A crisis doesn't make or break, it just
reveals.' When suffering comes, what is hidden in the heart will
be revealed. A person's faith may be tested and found to be less
strong than thought.
• A person who is connected to a church and engages in regular
worship and personal devotions will cope far better than
someone who is on the fringe of things. Bible teaching and
reflection can help to prepare Christians for tough times (Psa. 1;
John 15; James 1:2–8)
• What is defined as 'suffering' will vary from person to person
and depend on a host of factors including temperament,
frequency of crises in their life, expectations, state of health,
closeness to others – especially family.

How do we make sense of suffering?

Christians in crisis will often jump to asking 'Why?', seeking to make sense of an event or problem. This is especially the case when the suffering is apparently random – a sudden illness, an unexpected relationship break up, a financial setback, a random accident, unprovoked verbal or physical assault or untimely death.

The following answers are sometimes given:

- 'God has sent this to help you grow' (quoting Rom. 8:28: 'God works for the good of those who love him').
- 'God has sent this to punish you' (quoting Heb. 12:10: 'God disciplines us for our good').
- 'This is down to your own folly / sin.'
- 'The devil has sent this' (quoting 1 Pet. 5:8: 'the devil prowls around like a roaring lion').
- 'This is just part of the sad and random world we live in. Roll on heaven!'

Answering the 'Why?' question

All of us need to think through our own view of why suffering and crises may come. However, aiming to answer the question 'Why?' is generally inappropriate early on and though we may yearn to provide definitive answers, our knowledge is always partial and suggestions necessarily tentative. So although it may seem obvious, it is best not to suggest why something has happened simply in order to have something to reply.

Affirming the goodness and love of God in Christ

The question of suffering is only asked because we believe God to be good and all powerful. If God was like a dictator of a nation who was prone to random unpleasant outbursts against His own people then we wouldn't be asking the question. We would just assume that He was having a bad day and we don't need to think much more.

For most atheists, there is no expectation that there is any rhyme or reason to suffering. If you take a biblical God out of the equation then you are left to whatever philosophical framework you construct. In the case of many atheists, the assumption is that we are the product of blind chance through evolutionary process and so any suffering is the result of that randomness.

The Bible does not shirk away from the issue of suffering and yet constantly reminds us that God is love, God is good, He cares for people, He is not willing that any should perish, and He has good plans and purposes for the world. However, the reality of sin and its consequences (Gen. 3) are that Christians live in a fallen world where the enemy is at work. The nub of the issue is that God has created a world where the free will decisions of individuals have real consequences, which include suffering. We are born into this reality, are victims of it and, to some extent at least, contribute to it ourselves.

If God had enforced obedience to Him, as we might programme a robot, He could have ensured a suffering-free world, but the essence of life would be very different. He chose a world in which the exercise of free will led to Adam and Eve rejecting His way and inflicting us all with the sin virus that gives us a bias away from God, and towards self and self-interest. It mattered to God that we should freely choose to love Him, just as we know that you cannot force romantic love but delight in it being freely enjoyed and experienced. God thus prefers a world where suffering is a possibility because of the good that can come.

Bound up in this is the work of Satan whose entrance into the

Garden of Eden, and tempting of Eve, led to disobedience. So we have to get our minds around God allowing a fallen angel to have some influence in His world. While Satan mainly plays a relatively small role in the biblical narrative, his work is real. In the Old Testament, it is rare that events are attributed to Satan as such and even in the New Testament, where his work is more marked, the text doesn't major on him at all.

We conclude that God is all powerful but chooses to create a reality on Planet Earth where He doesn't control our actions but works His redemptive purposes in and through the work of human beings, and will one day bring things to a glorious completion when the whole cosmos is finally redeemed.

In some church traditions, there is an understanding that everything that happens is 'God's will', including suffering, because He intends it for His glory – and they might have Bible references to support their view. But this seems to contradict the view that God is good and will not promote evil. If we accept that God allows free choices then we have to accept that those choices may be evil. This doesn't make Him responsible for that evil, any more than parents, who have taught their children right from wrong, are to blame for any wrongdoings perpetrated by their offspring.

Whatever our view, we have to accept that God does not always choose to intervene when people suffer, and we will look at why in more detail a little later in the chapter.

The nature of God's redemptive work – the kingdom is now *and* not yet

Throughout the Bible, God intervenes in the affairs of humanity. When Adam and Eve sin, it is God who covers their nakedness and banishes them from the Garden of Eden. It is God who sends a flood to judge evil in the world and preserves Noah and his family. It is God who frustrates people at Babel by introducing languages into the world. It is God who calls Abram to follow Him and promises land, descendants and His blessing. It is God who preserves His people through famine, rescues them from Egypt and makes them a nation at Sinai. It is God who gives His law and leads His people to the Promised Land. It is God who is active in the lives of judges, kings and prophets that the world may know of His goodness and power. It is God who sends His people into exile and then brings them back. It is God who sends Jesus to us to reveal His love and bring His rule and reign afresh in the lives of His people. It is God who raised His son from the dead and sends His Spirit on all who would trust Him. It is God who directs the Church in this age to take the news of His love to the ends of the earth and will one day send His son back to earth to bring in the age to come where all who know and love Him will enjoy eternity in new bodies fitted for the new heavens and new earth.

So amidst the suffering and pain God *is* at work. We know that today He intervenes in the lives of people in response to prayer and through His own gracious provision. We see signs of His rule in the Church and give thanks for it. But we also see that God is at work in suffering too.

Value in suffering?

In any average week, most of us face some level of suffering. This may be very mild and barely worthy of the 'suffering' tag; for example, experiencing hunger and thirst for longer than we might like, being tired due to lack of sleep, coping with irksome coughs and colds, living with an ongoing physical complaint or aches and pains of advancing years. We may be troubled by what others have said about us or our perceived understanding of our role in the world. It is also right and good that we feel sadness and pain at what we see in the world around us – locally, nationally and internationally.

As we care for others, we seek to empathise with their pain whether it seems major or trifling to us. It can be deeply troubling if we spend any length of time caring for multiple people and see little progress. Seeing someone getting better might only be at the expense of a lot of our own time. But that is without heaven's perspective on suffering. Seen through a divine lens, we are better able to calibrate what is a win and what is a defeat. In short, any problem we face provides an opportunity for God to work.

In chapter 2, we saw how Jesus taught about the kingdom of God and how this kingdom overlaps with the present world where God's reign and rule are often not evident. But in the Sermon on the Mount, Jesus included the puzzling words: 'Blessed are you when people... persecute you' (Matt. 5:11). 'Blessed' can be translated to mean 'happy' and suggests that joy comes to those who are treated poorly because they follow Jesus. Jesus says that God will have His way of rewarding them. Indeed, later, the apostle Paul would warn Timothy that everyone who lives a godly life will be persecuted (2 Tim. 3:12). Paul wrote:

'Therefore, since we have been justified through faith, we have peace with God through our Lord Jesus Christ, through whom we have gained access by faith into this grace in which we now stand. And we boast in the hope of the glory of God. Not only so, but *we also glory in our sufferings, because we know that suffering produces perseverance*; perseverance, character; and character, hope. And hope does not put us to shame, because God's love has been poured out into our hearts through the Holy Spirit, who has been given to us.' (Rom. 5:1–5, emphasis added)

Paul saw sufferings as something that can be gloried in because of how they develop character in us. This is not masochistic; we are never encouraged to seek suffering but simply told that if it comes, we can be sure that things are happening.

James said something almost identical:

'Consider it pure joy, my brothers and sisters, whenever you face trials of many kinds, because you know that the testing of your faith produces perseverance. Let perseverance finish its work so that you may be mature and complete, not lacking anything.' (James 1:2–4)

Note that the apostles did not specify the source of the suffering or the reason for the suffering (although it is often read in terms of being a Christian). James' 'trials of many kinds' uses a Greek construction that embraces all manner of struggles whatever the source. Everything from losing our wallet to breaking a tooth; from struggling to please a boss to sleepless nights.

Paul was clearly confident in God's ability to be at work for our good, whatever comes and however unlikely:

'And we know that in all things God works for the good of those who love him, who have been called according to his purpose. For those God foreknew he also predestined to be conformed to the image of his Son, that he might be the firstborn among many brothers and sisters. And those he predestined, he also called; those he called, he also justified; those he justified, he also glorified.' (Rom. 8:28–30)

This passage tells us that God is at work for good in all things that we face because of His work of making us Christlike. God knows who will come to faith and these people are on a pathway to conformity to Christ.

In Paul's second letter to the Corinthians, we are taught that God Himself will draw near to us in our struggles and that His compassion to us will enable us to be of comfort to others:

'Praise be to the God and Father of our Lord Jesus Christ, the Father of compassion and the God of all comfort, who comforts us in all our troubles, so that we can comfort those in any trouble with the comfort we ourselves receive from God.' (2 Cor. 1:3–4)

Later Paul adds: 'For our light and momentary troubles are achieving for us an eternal glory that far outweighs them all' (2 Cor. 4:17). Paul believes that troubles can be a blessing under God's hand.

Suffering is normally seen as a part of life. Indeed, although some suffering comes as a result sin, you could argue that it is part and parcel of reality that there is some struggle. Just as a muscle strengthens through tension so we know that character development typically requires a modicum of struggle. The Hebrew writer reminds us that Jesus learnt obedience through what He suffered (Heb. 2:10). We become who we are through the choices we make. A contrary option to do evil is usually present for the option of choosing good to have meaning. There's no virtue in not getting drunk when no alcohol is available or not stealing when CCTV cameras are clearly monitoring us. Virtue is handing in a wallet containing £100 to the police or admitting doing something wrong when there were no witnesses. But what of the view that God has brought suffering to us in order to teach us something?

Below is an oft-quoted passage that speaks of God's disciplining us as His children:

> 'My son, do not make light of the Lord's discipline, and do not lose heart when he rebukes you, because the Lord disciplines the one he loves, and he chastens everyone he accepts as his son.' (Heb. 12:5–6)

Many teach that God sometimes orchestrates difficult situations in order to aid our growth in godliness; for example, a recurring or permanent illness, a job loss, a business collapse may result in us growing in our faith because we have to depend more on God.

The Hebrew writer uses the word *paideia* for discipline, which referred to the rearing of children through education. There are links of course with the training of a disciple, which is close to the English word 'discipline'. In this context, the writer is arguing that we are helped away from ignorance and incorrect behaviour and towards being correctly schooled in godly living.

As Christians, we acknowledge that we are in need of God's forgiveness and grace for our behaviour and need His help to live in keeping with His ways. In that sense, we know that all areas of life (blessings and sufferings) may teach us God's ways as we learn and grow daily. We needn't conclude that any particular event causing us to suffer has been sent by God, as if He was especially annoyed with us. But as suffering comes, we can thank Him for all that He will do in and through our challenges.

Suffering, therefore, is rarely due to our bad behaviour, which requires God to inflict something particular on us. Many with tender consciences would struggle under the double whammy of suffering and wondering how they have offended God. We are wise, of course, to confess sin and look for God's daily grace, regardless of whether suffering comes or not.

In some cases, we may be pretty sure that our pain is self-inflicted. We know that our actions or words have led to the pain we are facing. There's no doubt that this adds an additional trial to the unpleasant situation. But God will still work even when we have messed up. He is a good Father who enters our world and does all He can to ensure that things recover.

Whatever kind of suffering people are facing, as they come to Him in prayer, God will always be present and He will be at work, however tough that may seem or unlikely that will be.

There is much more that could be said on suffering. Some suffering does seem senseless and without any merit and this section might seem glib if you are facing situations where there seems to be no end and no value but we can hold fast to God's Word even if the 'value' isn't obvious.

General points when pastoring those who are suffering

1. We remember that Jesus was touched by suffering during His life and in His death. He experienced physical, emotional and spiritual suffering. He knows how we feel and can offer His grace at time of need.

2. We can have an attitude of confidence in God's purposes (James 1:3). The apostles encourage us to look to God's goodness in suffering.

3. Any crisis reminds us of the need to trust in God and not this world (Luke 13:22–30; 1 John 2:15–17). During Jesus' life, some Jews lost their lives at the hands of Pilate. They were caught up in a situation in the temple courts and died as a result. He was asked what He made of it and His reply was: 'unless you repent, you too will all perish' (Luke 13:3). He refuses to give an explanation but merely shows them that any

death is a reminder of our own mortality and we are wise to make provision for that time. Pain reminds us that this life is not the perfection that God intended and awaits us in the life to come.

4. We don't need to know 'Why?' in order to continue to look to God (Heb. 12:1–3). In the book of Job, we read about God's wager with Satan and see the pain and sadness that Job feels as he faces suffering with no idea why – and the book doesn't actually give us an answer. When Job finally hears from God, He reminds Job that He is the creator, that He is almighty and that Job (and indeed we) may not and will not understand fully all that God is doing.

5. Your mere presence will be a vital part of care – especially if others keep their distance because they don't know what to say. Job's friends are called 'comforters' with a touch of irony because their explanations did not help. They attempted to reason that his pain is some kind of 'karma' (my word) for what he had done, even though God had said, at the start of the book, that Job was upright and blameless. In most pastoral situations, the loving approach is to listen and provide practical help.

6. If the opportunity arises, we can reassure a person of God's love, understanding and desire to provide comfort and support. And though the initial shock and pain may make a faith response difficult, in time, it may be possible to talk about their need to respond in faith to God's goodness and care.

7. Praying with someone in need is a way to model an approach to the crisis. It is worth thinking what you might pray beforehand.

8. Some people may find prayer difficult, or be annoyed at God for what has happened. A faulty understanding of what the Christian faith is may be exposed by the crisis. In time, someone will need to provide gentle and loving teaching.
9. A crisis can breed a victim mentality: 'Why does it always happen to me?'
10. A crisis can breed jealousy: 'They never have problems!'

Consideration of these issues is vital, especially when the immediate pain of someone's situation is not at the forefront of our minds. It's worth thinking through the topic of suffering, so that if and when someone asks: 'If there is a God of love, why does He allow suffering?', our response is true to the God of love we worship, but also makes sense to others in their faith journey.

Questions to consider

• Think back to a time of suffering in your life. Do you recall your attitude towards God at the time?

_____

_____

• Is your response to suffering: 'No one knows why this has happened'? Or do your prefer to come up with some kind of explanation?

_____

_____

• How does knowing that Jesus suffered help you and those you care for?

_____

_____

07: Care for yourself as you care for others

It was while working for a student charity that I began to experience some serious health issues with my gut. At the local surgery, the doctor asked me about my lifestyle and I explained that I was travelling around the south east of England visiting Christian Unions in universities, covering maybe 1,000 miles a month and working around 70 hour weeks. He carefully explained that if I wanted to continue in that work, I would need to take it easier, and that the issues with my gut were directly due to the stress I was putting myself under. I am glad to say that with some help from a housemate and my boss, I adjusted my commitments and made time to play football, when I could, on Saturday mornings. It was a timely wake-up call and, by following the doctor's suggestions, I was able to serve for four years in that role.

It can be easy to forget to look after yourself. You have a heart that is keen to serve others. You understand the need to die to self and live for the cause of the gospel and so, like an intrepid explorer, you launch yourself into your work focused on care but with little thought to what caring for others may do to you. Many carers have found that the sprinting approach to caring was only sustainable for a season and a more measured approach was required. We saw in the introduction that many zealous Christian workers have become causalities because they failed to slow down. As a friend put it: 'You've got to look after your body. After all, where else would you live?!'

In caring for ourselves, it is a good idea to regularly reflect on these questions:

• What are the regular spiritual habits that keep you centred in God?

_____

• Are there any that you have intended to use, but never got round to?

_____

• How well do you use your time?

_____

• Do you regularly find yourself stretched? Is this something you can control?

_____

• In the last year, have there been times of weariness that are caused by overwork?

_____

- Have you found it easy to replenish yourself when you have had a tough pastoral interaction?

- Do you eat well?

- Do you drink enough fluids?

- Do you get enough sleep?

- Do you get enough rest and relaxation?

- Do you take at least one day a week as a rest day?

- Would you say you were a workaholic or more prone to laziness, or neither?

- How good are you at keeping to personal boundaries?

- Are there people who can keep an eye on your schedule and energy levels?

Having highlighted any areas for concern, you can then look at some methods and approaches that may help.

Identity in Christ

When thinking about caring for ourselves while in the service of others, we need to be clear and sure about our identity as beloved children of God, indwelt by God's Spirit and 'in Christ'. Much of western culture seeks to create identity from what we do, not who we are, and therein lies the subtle temptation to overwork in a vain attempt to earn the approval of God, who has already given it to us.

The eldest son in the parable of the prodigal son is instructive. His *modus operandi* is exposed when he responds angrily to the welcome received by the wayward son, and explains that he has been 'slaving' (Luke 15:29) for his father. The father points out that he would graciously share anything with the eldest son: '"My son," the father said, "you are always with me, and everything I have is yours"' (Luke 15:31). The slavish mindset, adopted by the eldest son, was all of his own making. In our care for others and ourselves, it is good to remember the abundance of life and grace that God provides for us in Christ.

Our identity in Christ is key because many care for others from other motivations, such as wanting to be liked, to be needed, to control people or believing to know best.

Of course, there is an element of self-interest in caring for others. There is a joy in service. It is more blessed to give than to receive, after all. But ideally, we care because of the joy and peace we have known in God, which spills out to those to whom we express love. This was Jesus' way and it can be ours too.

God central

The only template we have for pastoral ministry in the Bible is that provided by Jesus and the apostles demonstrated in the narrative of the Gospels and Acts and further insights in the epistles. There is no alternative biblical pastoral care! The New Testament pulsates with the life of God transforming situations as the kingdom, which the Jews thought would come at the end of time, was demonstrated in the here and now: sick people got better; the sad knew joy, the struggling were given courage. So the key issue we face in our pastoral care is the kind of God we serve and what we look for Him to do.

At one level you take yourself, such as you are, into your caring situation. You may feel weak, uncertain, ill-prepared and have 101 different ideas as to why you won't be any help.

But as you ask the Lord: what are You doing? How can I partner with You? How can Your grace be known in this situation? And remind yourself of the presence of God within the situation, you will find that, as with Elijah against the prophets of Baal on Carmel, you plus God equals a majority.

If you have a role and status in a church, this especially applies to you. Eugene Peterson said: 'they want a pastor they can follow so they won't have to bother following Jesus any more'[1]. If members of a church are following you – that's the first of their problems! Make sure they keep their eyes on God.

With our identity sorted, and our mind set on God, we are now ready to think about how we spend our time.

A wise understanding of time

Many people's time parameters are based on a working day of eight hours, which seems a reasonable average. And so carers might believe that they must measure their care in terms of time spent. For example, volunteering for four hours a week with four visits per hour (including travel time to and from) might seem a sensible measure. Except, of course, one visit is not comparable to another. Fifty minutes with one person might not feel like work at all, and you leave feeling richer for the experience and wondering when you can find an excuse to return. With others, 50 minutes can feel like three hours as you struggle to make sense of what they are saying and dodge issues that you know not to explore. You finish feeling absolutely drained, wondering whether you had been any help at all.

If you have ten pleasant visits, your energy expenditure will be very different than if you have ten challenging visits. It's helpful to have a wise perspective and build in compensations to your visits, like treating yourself to coffee and cake if your visit feels like 15 rounds with a Rottweiler!

You have your diary in hand. You have allotted time for pastoral care (whatever that means in your context). What are you going to do?

A sensible direction of energy

Triage is the practice of surveying a number of people with medical needs (say at a traffic accident) so that focused attention can be given to those critically ill, before attending to people with less serious injuries.

In the church world there are a multitude of needs. How do we decide on criteria for pastoral care intervention?

The following may seem common sense, but is frequently overlooked:

- Is the person already in a caring network, such as a home group, ministry, or friendship group?
- Do you know the person already and so have a prior connection that might assist the process?
- Is there a natural affinity in terms of age, interest, professional background?
- Would there be others on the team who might better assist them?

Someone may, of course, be determining your schedule for you. But even so, you can still give your own feedback and make suggestions before reflecting on your thought processes.

Developing mental strength

The New Testament reminds us that our thinking is key.

'Do not conform to the pattern of this world, but be transformed by the renewing of your mind. Then you will be able to test and approve what God's will is – his good, pleasing and perfect will.' (Rom. 12:2)

'For though we live in the world, we do not wage war as the world does. The weapons we fight with are not the weapons of the world. On the contrary, they have divine power to demolish strongholds. We demolish arguments and every pretension that sets itself up against the knowledge of God, and we take captive every thought to make it obedient to Christ.' (2 Cor. 10:3–5)

As we care, it is natural to ask ourselves: how did I do? Was the person helped? Could I have done better? Will I be able to cope in the future?

How we think about adversity, an event, or a series of events will have a major impact upon our response and ability to live wisely in the light of it. In chapter 5, we looked at Albert Ellis' ABC model[2] where: A = Activating event, B = Belief, and C = Consequent emotion. What we believe about an event will lead to the consequent emotion. You have to get to C from A via B.

This is especially important as we care for others and can easily mean interpreting matters incorrectly. For example, imagine you are walking down the street and see someone you know. They ignore you. If you believe they have done so deliberately, you may feel shunned and annoyed. But if you believe that they are upset or distracted, you will feel nothing yourself, and may feel sadness for them. These are two completely different emotional responses from the same 'Activating event', based on two different beliefs.

Ellis' model has been developed. You can add a 'D' and 'E', to change your emotions where: D = Dispute the belief and E = change Emotion.

Imagine this next scenario: someone sees their wife hugging a man who they don't know. What is the consequent emotion? It depends upon beliefs. Possible beliefs:

• She is having an affair. Emotion – betrayal, rage, anger.
• She has met someone she hasn't seen for a very long time. Emotion – peace, intrigue.
• She has just been saved from a mugging. Emotion – gratitude for the man's intervention.

What are your typical beliefs when an event (or series of events) takes place that overwhelms you? This will depend, to some extent, about our understanding of life in God. All that the Bible says about being a follower of God and His goodness can shape our mental outlook when we face circumstances that overwhelm us. This understanding can help us to focus on biblical truths and know peace as we commit our pastoral ministry to God.

Expanding emotional capacity

Depleting our emotional energy without sufficient recovery time can lead to unhelpful emotions, such as lack of confidence or impatience. In extreme times, burnout comes when our adrenal glands have been overactive to the point where they are unable to recover, leaving us unable to rise to the emotional needs we face.

Relationships can be the source of adversity but are part of our replenishment too in the form of honest reflection, sharing needs, receiving help, and offering help in the context of people who care for us. Paul advises: 'Carry each other's burdens, and in this way you will fulfil the law of Christ' (Gal. 6:2). Hence the questions earlier, do you have good quality renewal time? How much of your time are you relaxed (other than sleeping)?

But remember also that for a muscle to grow it needs to be put 'under stress', so by analogy a little emotional stress can enable us to expand our emotional capacity. Maybe you have been stretched, but glad you were.

The importance of boundaries

Anyone who is engaged in pastoral care will discover the importance of boundaries. For some people, this is literally the difference between lasting a few months and having a long and fruitful ministry. A boundary is a personal property line that marks those things for which we are responsible. Boundaries define who we are and who we are not.

One pastoral carer, known to me, gave a mobile phone number to someone they were caring for and received calls at all times of the day and night. He had sympathy for the person in need, but knew that their pestering approach wasn't helping either of them. He changed his mobile number pretty quickly.

Examples of helpful boundaries:

- Time and place limitations on availability of the pastoral carer are essential.
- Boundaries regulating contact of the carer at home need to be fixed and maintained.
- The carer must never allow the person being cared for to control the process.
- Carers should be able to recognise when they are out of their depth and refer the individual to someone else.
- If carers become emotionally overwhelmed or enmeshed in a person's issues, they need to seek advice.
- Confidentiality boundaries should also be understood. Never promise that you will not disclose anything to another. A useful general guideline is: confidentiality will be maintained unless there is a risk of the person being cared for harming themselves or others, or being harmed by another person.
- Agreed expectations between yourself and church leaders regarding what you should disclose to them about those you care for.

These guidelines may seem a little stark in black and white and can of course be adjusted for crises. Problems do not fit set times. But there's a difference between occasional interruptions and a life of permanent chaos. When the irregular becomes the rule, you know you need to get some structure into your day.

Reasons for having boundaries include:

- Needing times for rest and recuperation.

- Needing times that friends and family know you are fully present with them.
- Helping those you care for receive help from others, or manage themselves.
- Giving you margin for times of personal crisis and illness.

Meeting people

Once you have your boundaries in place, it's time to think about the details of meeting and chatting with people. Wise points to bear in mind when meetings with clients[3]:

- Consider the setting: is it safe, open, populated, quiet and uncompromising?
- Consider inviting a third person for an initial meeting, or if you are unsure about safety. Be aware of and close to exits.
- Carry a mobile phone or some means of contacting support, even if meeting in a neutral area or visiting someone well known to you.
- Be aware of issues of sexual attraction and co-dependency. If necessary, make sure that other arrangements are made for their support, or meet with others present.
- It's wise to ensure that home visits are diarised, and that a third party knows about your meeting.
- Try to stick to the pre-agreed timeframe for pastoral meetings: ideally no more than 50 minutes.
- Have a developed strategy for responding to client crisis calls or breaching of normal boundaries.
- Ensure confidentiality is maintained.
- Explain to the client the structures of reporting and supervision, who will be kept informed etc.
- Never offer personal details of other team members unless permission has been granted to do so.

Teamwork

I appreciate that not every reader of this book works in a team. Attendees at courses I run are often the only person who is doing formal caring in their church. But the ideal is that we work towards having a small team, which includes someone who oversees the work.

Pastoral care co-ordination:

1. Ideally a co-ordinator monitors visits and checks that all is well.
2. Newcomers to care are given a short probationary period ending with a review and opportunity to mutually agree to continue or stop.
3. Regular carers are trained and encouraged to adopt wise practices.
4. People with more training and expertise (eg qualified counsellors, psychiatrists, doctors) can be identified to be involved. It may be possible to involve other networks (family, friends, small group members) who may offer additional supportive care.
5. The agreement and comfort level of the person being cared for has to be taken into account in decisions relating to how care will be provided. This is in order to avoid unforeseen problems (eg in certain situations, the involvement of close family may be inappropriate, but the small group may be mobilised to assist).
6. The team can be brought together as often as is needed: to pray for one another, advise one another (while protecting confidence) and share burdens.
7. The co-ordinator can assess whether carers need other carers to replace them or join them, especially if they are finding the needs of anyone particularly challenging.

It is good practice to see other carers as a resource, which is why I advocate having carers meet with the rest of the team on a regular basis (at least monthly) in order to talk through how it's going and, where necessary, adjust the approach. The content of conversation needs to be respectful of confidences, but ideally people cared for will know that matters may be brought to a wider team, which should be good for all concerned. I have known carers become enmeshed in the lives of people in a way that is detrimental to them. Some people's situations can seem overwhelming and a carer not versed in manipulative interpersonal relations may well find that one person can hijack their whole care ministry.

Temptation

We all face temptations from time to time. The nature of the caring role can mean we become emotionally attached to those we care for, which is why it is generally considered advisable for men to support other men and women to support other women. (Where same-sex attraction exists, perhaps another approach may be adopted). Accountability is hugely important.

It can be tempting (pun intended) to focus on the more obvious areas of temptation. Richard Foster's book, *Money, Sex and Power*[4] detailed these key areas for the Christian and perhaps especially the Christian leader. We can easily assume we are immune, only to find a person, circumstance or opportunity that entices us more than we realise. Resolving this requires more space than we have but within the context of this chapter, we note that we are more susceptible to temptation when we fail to care for ourselves and see extra money, abusing power or sexual relations as a 'relief'.

Sin takes many forms and we will all have our weaker areas: gossip, pride and envy may not be Foster's top three, but unchecked will create havoc in our lives too. We are wise to keep short accounts with God and be constantly glad of God's faithfulness in welcoming us back when we stray.

Safeguarding
Every church should have a safeguarding policy. A safeguarding or child protection policy is a statement that outlines what an organisation or group will do to keep children safe.

It should include:
- A statement setting out the organisation's commitment to protecting all children.
- What the organisation will do to keep children safe and respond to concerns.
- A list of the supporting procedures that accompany the policy.

If you need help in framing or updating one then there are places that you can contact. The ACC website (acc-uk.org) will have some material and if your church is part of a denomination, someone will have done the thinking for you.

Spirit empowered living
One of the chief antidotes to stress and burnout is to have a personal sense of what you are doing for God and in Jesus' name.

People inside and outside the Church see the value of the inner life: a sense of purpose that drives us forward and explains why we live. The key muscle that fuels spiritual energy is character: the courage and conviction to live by our values, even if this means personal sacrifice and hardship.

Self-absorption drains us of energy and prevents us from performing well. Having a mission to work for helps to take us out of ourselves and put our best efforts to a greater purpose.

There is sometimes a tension between who we are and who we want to be, and this can feel overwhelming. But in God's purposes, this is a healthy tension. Jesus brings His followers into challenging situations, to stretch them so they can grow, and this can include our pastoral care load.

Remember that our spiritual lives were designed to be refreshed in God. 'My people have committed two sins: They have forsaken me, the spring of living water, and have dug their own cisterns, broken cisterns that cannot hold water' (Jer. 2:13).

When we think about caring for ourselves, once again Jesus is our model. He was fully God and fully man and engaged in practices that helped Him stay refreshed as He served. Many would argue that if *He* needed spiritual habits, how much more do we!

'A farmer is helpless to grow grain; all he can do is provide the right conditions for the growing of grain. He cultivates the ground, he plants the seed, he waters the plants, and then the natural forces of the earth take over and up comes the grain… This is the way it is with the Spiritual Disciplines – they are a way of sowing to the Spirit… By themselves the Spiritual Disciplines can do nothing; they can only get us to the place where something can be done.'[5]

Spiritual practices help to create the conditions where we give God the opportunity to empower us. For example, fasting from food helps to develop self-control, so that we are better able to handle other areas where we may be tempted towards excess. They are an intentionally directed action by which we act in our power in order to receive from God the ability (or power) to do what we cannot do by direct effort.

Many people claim not to be able to run a marathon but if they are fit and healthy enough, most could. They just need to commit themselves to the training, so that their bodies become capable of running 26 miles 385 yards.

None of us can walk like Jesus did. But if we put in the training (engage in the spiritual practices), over time God will do His work so that we can.

The inward practices

• Meditation: mulling over the Word of God, often involving memorising key phrases.
• Prayer: conversation with God about our life together.
• Fasting: the giving up of something – normally food – so that we can more easily receive from God.
• Study: concerted time focusing on the Bible and books about the Bible so that we better understand what is being said.
• Sabbath: the setting aside of time for refreshment and spiritual renewal (Sundays for most believers).

The outward practices (inward realities resulting in outward lifestyles)

• Simplicity: paring life down to the bare essentials by getting rid of clutter.
• Solitude: spending significant periods of time alone (one hour minimum) and in silence so that we can catch up with ourselves and God.
• Submission: laying down the burden of needing to get our own way; being willing to accept another's authority or choices, especially God's whom we ultimately serve.
• Service: willingly working for others, often in secret, knowing that it is God whom we ultimately serve.

The corporate practices (activities we typically do with others)

- Confession: expressing our sins and failings to God and, where necessary, to each other.
- Worship: the conscious living of all of life in praise to God, including praise in word and song with other Christians.
- Spiritual direction: seeking God's help as we live our life, listening to the voice of His Spirit and counsel from His people.
- Celebration: the enjoyment of God and life in play and laughter, dancing and food, according to the preferences of the group we are with.

Spiritual practices needn't be seen as a burden, or another list of things you don't do and feel guilty about; they are means of grace and you probably do many already. If you are to care for yourself, you need to receive the grace of God and these habits will help you put yourself in the way of His grace. That way, when the crisis comes, you are breathing God-like air and can have the energy to care in Jesus' name for whoever needs it.

Questions to consider

- Which practices are you going to utilise to make sure you are going to care for yourself as God intends?

_____

_____

_____

• Which areas of life do you need to work on to ensure that you can truly care for yourself as you care for others?

_____

_____

• Is there someone who could keep you accountable to whatever you decide?

_____

_____

[1] Marva Dawn and Eugene Peterson, _The Unnecessary Pastor_ (Grand Rapids, MI, USA: Eerdmans, 2000) p4
[2] A. Ellis, 'Rational Psychotherapy and Individual Psychology', _Journal of Individual Psychology_, Vol 13, 1957, pp38–44
[3] Adapted from Will van der Hart, 'Draft Pastoral Care Policy for Churches or Organisations', posted 25 March 2017, taken from mindandsoulfoundation.org [Accessed March 2019]
[4] Richard Foster, _Money, Sex and Power_ (London: Hodder & Stoughton, 2009)
[5] Richard Foster, _Celebration of Discipline: The Path to Spiritual Growth_ (London: Hodder & Stoughton, 2008)

08: Learn wise caring practices

Criminologists are aware of the 'Locard Exchange Principle' named after Dr Edmond Locard who formulated a basic principle of forensic science, summed up by the maxim 'every contact leaves a trace'. Reflecting on the perpetrator of a crime, he said: 'Wherever he steps, whatever he touches, whatever he leaves, even unconsciously, will serve as a silent witness against him. Not only his fingerprints or his footprints, but his hair, the fibers from his clothes, the glass he breaks, the tool mark he leaves, the paint he scratches, the blood or semen he deposits or collects. All of these and more, bear mute witness against him. This is evidence that does not forget. It is not confused by the excitement of the moment. It is not absent because human witnesses are. It is factual evidence. Physical evidence cannot be wrong, it cannot perjure itself, it cannot be wholly absent. Only human failure to find it, study and understand it, can diminish its value.'[1]

A strange principle to introduce to a book on pastoral care perhaps! But a reminder that if the perpetrator of a crime 'leaves a trace' so do you and I when we connect with people. If we are looking to make some marginal gains in pastoral care then improving the abilities of each carer would be vital. We want our contact with a person cared for to be full of God's love and grace and an opportunity to express love to them in the name of Jesus so that they may find, deepen, and develop their faith in Him.

Obviously, the context of care will vary and may occur between friends and family, and so not known in a formal way. This chapter focuses on what is traditionally known as a 'pastoral visit' where someone designated by a church meets with someone who has asked for a visit or is deemed to need a visit by those concerned about them and may take place in a home, or appropriate public place.

Let's imagine that I am meeting Rob, a 25-year-old guy. His name has been passed to me as needing a visit. I check the address and discover he lives three miles away from me. Let's walk through my visit to him.

Reason for visit

In most cases, a pastoral visit comes because of some kind of need expressed. You are visiting because the person, or someone close to the person, has expressed a need for a visit. Make no mistake, the mere fact that you are paying a visit will generally be appreciated. You represent the church and the other pastors in some way and help the person feel noticed and valued.

There will be some suggestion given as to why the visit needs to be made, and it is worth gaining as much information as you can at this stage. But bear in mind that the presenting problem may mask a deeper need or further needs, and not all the facts may be initially apparent.

People who typically require visiting are:
• The hospitalised
• The elderly and infirm

- Those who have been ill for a while
- The bereaved
- Members of the church who haven't attended for a while
- Those who are discouraged
- Newcomers
- Families of children or young people

Some of these will be one-off visits, some will be ongoing. You may visit the same people regularly or be one of many people who make pastoral visits.

In this case, I have no idea why Rob wants a visit so I phone up and make an appointment.

'Hi Rob, this is Andy Peck from the church.'

'Oh, hi Andy.'

'I'm not sure we have met?'

'I recognise your name. You preach from time to time?'

'That's right. I am also on the pastoral care team, and your name was passed to me as needing a visit. Does that make any sense to you?'

'Oh yes, that's fine. When can you come over?'

'I was wondering if Tuesday afternoon would be alright. But wasn't sure if you would be at work?'

'I work shifts, and am off then, so that's fine.'

'Can you give me an idea of why you'd like a visit?'

'Just been feeling a bit down. Thought I had better tell someone.'

'Oh, I'm sorry to hear that. Did you need to talk at all now on the phone?'

'Nah. Just a bad patch, I guess.'

'OK. Well, call the church office if you need to contact me beforehand. But if not, I look forward to catching up with you on Tuesday at 2pm, OK?

'Yes, sure. See you then.'

Are you going alone?

As a matter of good practice, I let the church office know that I am meeting Rob at 2pm for a chat. In this case, it's fine to go alone. Rob is known to the church and not likely to be awkward. If it wasn't Rob but Roberta, I would certainly have gone with someone else, or suggested that someone else visits her. I could also have met her at the church office, depending on the nature of the meeting.

Pray beforehand and during

My basic attitude is that I may not always be able to help, but I know that God can. I look to Him. So all the time, I am committing the visit to God. 'Lord, please draw near to Rob even now and enable this conversation to be of value in Your purposes.'

Clarify expectations

Rob knows what the pastoral care team is about, and so it will be clear what is offered. But in your case, you may need to clarify. If you are the pastor, there may be assumptions on both sides as to what you are doing. In some churches today and in many settings in the past, the pastoral visit had a degree of solemnity attached to it, especially if such visits were rare. As the assistant pastor in one church, I was aware that I was a poor substitute for 'the pastor'!

You may see your role as pastoral counselling, as a 'soul carer' or a teacher of the Word, and seek to do that within the visit alongside praying for the person. If you are visiting as a member of a church's pastoral care team, it is a good idea to clarify in your own mind what you are doing and what you are not doing.

Pastoral visiting is not in itself discipling, counselling, or offering spiritual direction. If you have expertise in these fields, that is something that could be offered, but in terms of the pastoral visit, your focus is the wellbeing of the person and seeing what may be needed.

We have noted in a previous chapter why problems arise and you will want to be keen to spot what's going on and provide what care you can, whether this be in terms of the care you give in the visit, or care you initiate subsequently.

Your approach

It may be obvious but it's worth saying that as you visit, you will be careful to respect the rights and dignity of every person as a unique individual, equal with them in the sight of God and regardless of race, religion, nationality, language, gender, marital status, sexual orientation, age, size, employment, income, disability, health, abode, or criminal record. You are not there to make judgments on life choices or sexual preferences. It's not irrelevant and you're equally not saying 'anything goes!' but in the context of your care, you are there to listen and understand. Of course, if you are asked about what the Bible says about something, then this may be something you want to chat about sometime.

It's helpful to remember that visiting doesn't mean having all the answers or making it all better, but is a means to humbly and prayerfully seek ways to help, knowing that God has all the solutions.

I knew that Rob was feeling down but had no idea whether he was understating something that was much worse and might need medical attention or counselling, or whether something bad had triggered his mood, which he would eventually recover from. I also had no idea how often he felt down.

The conversation

I ring the door bell and Rob invites me in.

I look for cues for something to chat about. He has a paintbrush in his hand so I start there.

> *'Hi Rob!'*
>> 'Hi Andy, thanks for coming.'
>
> *'Decorating eh?'*
>> 'Well, just touching up a door that needed it.'
>
> *'You enjoy that kind of thing?'*
>> 'Not really.'
>
> *'Have you decorated the house yourself?'*
>> 'I did a bit when we first moved in, but in the end we got a mate in who has his own business.'
>
> *'You say "we"?'*
>> 'Yeah, me and the missus. This is our first home. We were renting down East Street and this came up when we started looking.'
>
> *'Oh, great. Seems like a quiet neighbourhood.'*
>> 'You should be here when next door's dog's barking! But yeah, it's pretty quiet.'

It has to be said that this kind of 'small talk' is vital. It can be concerning the person's home, the people who live there, the weather, anything major in the news, or recent events at the church.

It was time to clarify the purpose for being there.

'So Rob, good to have this chance to see you and hear
more about how things are. You said on the phone
you were feeling down?'
'That's right.'

When writing a news story as a journalist, I was taught to use the elements mentioned in Rudyard Kipling's famous poem:

'I keep six honest serving-men
(They taught me all I knew);
Their names are What and Why and When
And How and Where and Who'.

It's not a bad aide-memoir as you seek to clarify things and work out what to say.

• What has happened?
• When did it happen (or start)?
• Where did it happen?
• Who was involved?
• How did it happen?
• Why do you think it happened? (Considering 'why' may or may not be appropriate as we may be considering motives, which may not be known or understood, or medical matters that may not be established or knowable.)

So I follow up my initial question by asking: 'When did you start to feel down?'

Rob explained that he had been feeling rubbish for a good few months. He doesn't really know why and can't think of anything particular that triggered it.

'Does this affect your work?'

    'Some days I can barely face work.'

'What do you do?'

    'I am a paramedic.'

'Ah, hence the shift work?'

    'That's right.'

'I am guessing you have to be pretty tough to do that kind of work?'

    'Yes. We see some stuff. Just part of the job.'

'You been doing it long?'

    'Twelve months. I was in retail before and much prefer this. Feel I am doing something that matters.'

'It may seem an obvious question but was there a call out that especially affected you?'

    'Like I said. I don't think so.'

'And is "feeling down" something that happens often?'

    'Not really, we all have ups and downs, but this is new to me.'

Listening

My role in the conversation was clearly to listen to what Rob was facing.

Listening may sound simple, but it isn't always easy. You may be tempted to speak, or interject, or counsel, but the initial role is hearing what they have to say in an open-handed and non-judgmental way.

'Just as love of God begins with listening to His Word, so the beginning of love for the brethren begins with listening to them.'[2]

Listening with our whole person

You may have met people who have a habit of looking elsewhere during a conversation. It might seem like they have someone better to talk to, or place to be, rather than with you.

Our body language when we are with someone conveys a lot. You don't want to be gazing into their eyes, and some conversations may be easier walking, but you do need to make eye contact from time to time.

Our posture, body language, gestures and facial expressions are all part of how we communicate non-verbally. Don't worry, you don't need to be perfecting acting skills, just be aware that how you appear will have an effect. If you are not sure how you typically come across to others (and many are totally unaware), it may be worth chatting with a good friend.

I discovered that I would be almost too attentive and make a high pitched murmur when someone spoke, because I wanted them to know I was listening. But it wasn't a good effect and thankfully friends told me it was irritating.

Listening to the whole person – verbal and non-verbal

Professor Abraham Mehrabi's study[3] on implicit communication is often quoted. Below are some of his findings:

- 7% of message pertaining to feelings and attitudes is in the words that are spoken.
- 38% of message pertaining to feelings and attitudes is paralinguistic (the way that the words are said).
- 55% of message pertaining to feelings and attitudes is in facial expression.

The point is well made that if we focus purely on what someone says we are likely to miss a good deal of what they are conveying.

In Rob's case, the body language did not tell me, 'I am depressed' even though his words had. It was too early to tell if that meant he really was OK, or had been able to pull himself together for our meeting. But there was definitely a marked contrast between his words and his general demeanour.

Listening to the voice

When visiting a person in need of pastoral care, try listening to their tone of voice, pitch, level, intensity. If you don't know them well, you won't have any previous behaviour to match with and may not know whether how they sound is typical or not. But you will get some idea and most of us intuitively pick things up.

I thought Rob sounded OK and together. He was even animated at times, as if talking about someone else, which seemed strange when I knew he felt depressed.

Listening to the silences

Don't feel you have to fill in the silences, especially if they come after you have asked a question. They may need time to reflect, and a minute of time, though it may seem awkward, can be valuable for them.

Listening to the thinking

As you listen, you may discover common words, themes or attitudes that are being replayed.

Rob mentioned his wife quite a lot. It made me think that they must be very close, but in a first meeting, I didn't like to probe.

It can be helpful to reflect back what is heard, even paraphrasing the words heard so the person knows they have been listened to.

It may seem odd, but them hearing the actual words is reassuring. However, don't overdo it!

Asking questions

It was Eugene Kennedy who said: 'The counsellor who wants to understand others is well advised to count to ten before asking any questions at all.'[4]

A pastoral carer is not always a counsellor as well, but it is helpful to know how to conduct an appropriate conversation. As a carer, your role is to best understand what is happening and what the needs are and explore the subject in hand. Some types of questioning could imply that you are asking in order to provide some kind of analysis, so it's wise to restrict your questions to ones that help you better understand their needs.

You may have a hundred questions but caring does not give you the right to be nosey. Wise questioners will always aim for open questions not closed ones, such as 'How are you coping?' rather than 'You must be struggling?'

Being specific

Sometimes people find it difficult to be specific – they may feel embarrassed for themselves or for others about what has happened or how they are feeling. At times, we may need to help people move on by either tentatively putting into words what we think is the situation or asking them for clarification. This needs to be done sensitively and in an environment of trust.

In Rob's case, using the 'Six honest serving men' poem was all I needed to do to explore what concerned him and give him a chance to talk.

Advising

Times of need can give rise to a whole host of spiritual questions; for example, why did God allow this? Where is God in this? Is God trying to teach me something? What should I do now?

People in need may perceive that your role as a carer gives you some kind of hotline to heaven. We have looked at the subject of suffering earlier in the book, and it may be necessary to gently assure them that God has not brought suffering into their lives, but that God will use whatever they are going through. In extreme cases, this may sound glib and unfeeling and you may want to keep your words to a minimum. Stand firm on the love of God, on our trust in Him and the value of ongoing prayer and you won't go far wrong.

With Rob I was trying to assess a few things. Is this 'being down' a big issue that might need a counsellor or medication? I am not trained as a counsellor or doctor, so it's not for me to delve into that area. Instead I asked:

'Have you tried anything to help you out of this bad patch?'

'Well, I pray but that doesn't seem to do any good.'

'Sorry to hear that. God hears us but sometimes His healing process can take a while. Anything else?'

Rob shrugged his shoulders.

It was time to tell Rob what I thought the next stage might be.

'Rob, look, I think it's great that you have asked to see someone and I want to be there for you through this. It may be that you are going through a season that will soon pass. But it may be helpful to see a friend of mine who is attached to the church who can give you more insight than I can.'

I paused, hoping he might say something or give me an indication of whether he liked the idea or not.

> 'What, like a counsellor?
>
> 'Yes.'
>
> 'Not sure I would want that. We don't have money for that kind of thing.'
>
> *'Don't worry about that. If that's what you need, we can sort that out. But look, if that's a big step, let's leave it and maybe we can touch base next Tuesday?'*

I was reluctant to give Rob advice because I didn't exactly know where the real issue lay. It would take a few more visits for me to establish that the source of him 'feeling down' was that his relationship with his wife was struggling. This was the reason he kept talking about her: not that they were close at that point in time. Maybe this was unconscious or maybe he knew it all along and hoped I would pick it up, when I probed.

At that point, I advised Rob and his wife, Sally, to chat with someone, and thankfully they did.

Praying

Most of the time, it will be appropriate to pray with the person you visit. You will sense whether you both pray or you just pray for them. This is not just a good routine to adopt but a precious and vital act as you invite God into the situation or further talk with Him about the situation.

It might also be appropriate to pray for healing in Jesus' name, if this is something you are familiar with. If they don't sense anything or aren't healed – reassure them of your ongoing prayers.

If you are at a hospital bed, it may be that others can hear your prayers, so be mindful of that. You don't want to embarrass your patient but equally you don't want to miss an opportunity to express truth in your prayer, which may benefit other listeners.

Sharing Scripture

Sharing a psalm or passage from the Bible might be apposite for a particular pastoral visit depending on your relationship with the person and their stage of faith. A more relaxed method is to share something that you have been learning or reading with a brief comment. You could do so as you pray or along with prayer; for example, 'Well, it would be good to pray. I was reading some verses from 1 Peter the other day, which might be of interest...'

During my time with Rob, sharing something from the Bible didn't seem appropriate, but on other occasions, it has worked well.

Ending

As a rule, it's better to stay too little than too long. They may be happy to talk for a very long time and, if you know them well and have the time, that isn't a bad thing. But it's appropriate for you to bring things to a close, and signal that you are about to leave.

I have condensed my actual conversation with Rob, which was actually around 40 minutes and seemed the right amount of time for someone I hadn't met before.

Follow up

Actions following a pastoral care visit might include:
• Arranging a rota for meals to be delivered.
• Getting in touch with a debt counsellor.
• Arranging a reconciliation meeting with another person.

• Praying.

• Checking up on them via phone or text in a few days.

• Getting in touch after they have had a hospital appointment.

Your visit will be valuable but lack of follow-up care diminishes its value. Indeed, it may make it worse – 'I shared my heart with you but you didn't care!'

It was very important that Rob and I met the following week, and that I recalled what we chatted about and revisited the possibility of him seeing a counsellor. It was on my third visit that the marriage issues surfaced, and he and Sally agreed to see someone in church who specialised in marriage guidance.

You will need to be careful about making any notes during and after the visit, but I find it useful to make some notes that I can refer to before the next visit. It matters that you remember the names of family or key people in their life, which sports team they follow and how they take their hot drinks. Data protection means that we keep any notes under lock and key and without any identification; use annotation if necessary.

Evaluating

This is particularly relevant when you have been supporting someone in a pastoral situation over a period of time. Being able to stand back and see what might have changed can be a great encouragement and bring hope for further change. It also gives the opportunity to discuss with the person in need whether the time has come for your supportive role to change.

You will need to be especially aware of how those you help can become emotionally attached to you. Good pastoral care cannot be free of some sense of people valuing what you do for them and looking forward to your visit. You may be a 'shoulder to cry on', a confidante, a sounding board, or a friend. But it's tricky when the person perceives you in a way that you don't perceive them. Your love for them means that you are seeking their wellbeing and this should typically mean that they build connections with a wide range of people, not just you. It is not healthy if someone cared for has excessive focus on one pastoral carer, and what we said in the last chapter about boundaries applies here.

As I evaluated things with Rob, I felt a little foolish that it took me three visits before he was able to share that it was a problem in the marriage that was making him feel down. But I didn't reproach myself. I was there to express love in the name of Jesus, not solve his problems. If he needed three weeks, that was fine. I was glad to be of some help and, in time, their relationship improved.

Questions to consider

- If you have been engaged in pastoral visits, what would you like to improve?

_____

_____

- Reflect back on pastoral meetings you have had. What has pleased you? What do you think the people you visit would say about the meetings?

_____

_____

• Is there anyone who you could usefully learn from? Why not arrange for a coffee and chat?

[1]Paul L. Kirk, *Crime investigation: physical evidence and the police laboratory* (New York, USA: Interscience Publishers, 1953)
[2]Dietrich Bonhoeffer, *Life Together* (Danvers, MA: SCM Press, 2015)
[3]Albert Mehrabian, *Silent messages: Implicit communication of emotions and attitudes* (Belmont, CA, USA: Wadsworth, 1981)
[4]Eugene Kennedy and Sara C. Charles, *On Becoming a Counsellor: A Basic Guide for Counsellors and Other Helping Professions* (Mahwah, NJ, USA: Paulist Press, 2017)

Part
3

Essential
strategy

09: Structure care appropriately

Chip and Dan Heath's bestselling book, *Made to Stick*[1], has helped many reflect on how communication works. The brothers talk about what they call 'the curse of knowledge', a phrase that seems very odd initially but explains how we easily forget what it's like to not know what we know and that this becomes like a curse.

They quote the work of a Stanford University graduate student of psychology named Elizabeth Newton, who in 1990 illustrated the curse of knowledge by studying a simple game. She asked people to adopt the role of 'tapper' and 'listener'. The tapper would tap the rhythm of a well-known song such as 'Jingle Bells' and it was the listener's job to ascertain the song. Over the course of Newton's experiment, 120 songs were tapped out.

How many songs do you think were correctly guessed? The answer is just three (2.5%). However, when the tappers were asked what proportion were guessed, they predicted 50%. Newton concluded that the curse of knowledge was the reason for this: tappers knowing the tune they are playing are unable to imagine what the listeners are hearing. They hear the tune in their head but it is poorly represented by mere taps on the table.

Our perspective of our church is shaped by 'insider knowledge': what is in our head (the melody of the church if you will) makes the internal workings of the church and its members clear to us. We forget that on many weeks (maybe every week), someone is new and doesn't have a clue what is going on, what to expect or what the church is about. We think we are being welcoming to newcomers, when in fact we are doing things that make them feel alienated. Consequently, unless they are prepared to persist through the awkwardness, newcomers don't come back. And a church wonders why it isn't growing!

This chapter looks at how we can structure a church so that people can receive what they need for where they are at in their faith journey.

There is a five-phase model of pastoral care (originally used by Ron Kallmier) for local congregations:

1. Entry
2. Connecting
3. Care and support
4. Equipping
5. Releasing into mission

It is helpful from a planning and strategy perspective to view the five phases as sequential, though in reality they do always not operate in that way. People may 'move around' among phases two to five, depending on their individual circumstances.

People may be located in more than one phase at a time. For example, they may be reconnecting after a year's absence from the church because of a work move, but they may also be involved in phase five (eg fulfilling duties within the local church or representing the presence of Jesus within their workplace or their local community). Phase three may be necessary at any point of time with any individual, given life's uncertainties.

Phase one: entry

Entry describes the pathway(s) for people to come into the life of the local church. Those who are new may fit one of the following categories:
- Those who have little or no church background.
- Those who come with negative church experiences or major reluctance in coming.
- Those who are just checking the church out.
- Those who are seeking a new church.
- Those who want to remain anonymous.
- Those who are or are becoming disciples of Jesus Christ.
- Those who are alone.
- Those who come with others.
- Those who are new but not for the first time.

Typically, we may imagine someone's first contact with a church to be at a service but this could include any gatherings of the church or part of the church.

How do people enter your church? How do we make things as easy as possible for someone to 'enter' the life of the church?

First church visit
The best way of helping newcomers is for a church member to chat with them one to one. Engendering a welcoming mentality helps everyone realise it's 'their job'. But in larger churches, it is not

easy to spot newcomers, and in any case many newcomers want to be anonymous – they don't especially want to be buttonholed, especially if they are investigating faith. Some deliberately choose larger churches so they can slip in and out unnoticed.

Many churches have ways in which newcomers can indicate their desire to connect via a welcome card. Some will give a welcome pack, which explains more about the church. They can indicate an openness to further contact via text of email. Other churches have a welcome desk, where newcomers can sign up for information or opportunities for connection.

A newcomer's tea, hosted by someone on the church leadership, gives a chance for the direction of the church to be explored and people to become known in more depth. In time, churches with a membership approach can share their values and vision with newcomers.

Some people's first experience of church may be through a seekers' course such as Alpha, Christianity Explored or the Y Course. Following these courses, there might be candidates for baptism, who usually attend a short preparation course in a small group setting. Praying for all these first entry points for newcomers will hopefully be a prayer team that people can approach for individual personal needs.

Phase two: connecting

The connecting phase is how a church arranges for people to build relationships with one another, to identify with the church family and thus develop a sense of belonging.

The weekly church gathering

The best kind of connection arises naturally from people meeting one another in a natural way. People discover things in common, are introduced to other people, share stories and activities of mutual interest. This kind of interaction takes place the world over in a myriad of situations without organisation. Often the time constraints before and after a service make it trickier for this to happen naturally, especially in a larger church. A regular church member's focus might be directed on people who are friends and acquaintances, while people who are outsiders might feel awkward, stood on their own. Sometimes a church is convinced it's 'friendly' when actually that is code for 'friendly to people we know'!

Just as pastoral care is everyone's job but in practice has to be arranged by the few, welcoming new people is everyone's responsibility but natural connections might organically happen within a smaller circle of people.

Small groups

Small groups have been seen as 'the answer' to all church ills, everything from lack of intimacy to world poverty! But there is no doubt that gatherings of a small number of people over a period of time can create connection. It has always been a key way for friendships to develop. Small groups are set up for a number of things but even if their focus is on learning about the Bible, good connection is a by-product. Creating groups worth joining can be tricky and I tackle this in my book, *Small Group Essentials*[2], if you need some guidance.

Ministry connections

Later in this chapter, we will be looking at how Christians need to see themselves as apprentices of Jesus who have a ministry themselves. But for now, we note that there is nothing like a common service or ministry to encourage community. In the same way that people who go on a mission trip for a week become lifelong friends, you probably know that your best connections are with people who you serve in the trenches with.

Home visit

It may be regarded as 'old school' but some churches would still send a staff member, delegated person or even the pastor to pay a visit to people who have filled in a welcome card. This may have a number or purposes, one of which would be helping the individual, couple or family to connect with the church family.

Social events

You can facilitate connections by arranging events that have a broad interest for people, for example: barn dance, ramble, potluck supper, karaoke, board games evening, talent show, barbecue, Wii challenge night, clean the church Saturday, craft evening, kite flying day, car care clinic or picnic.

Website

Make sure your website is up to date with information of what's on and who to contact. If your church website has the facility, upcoming events can be flagged up on the home page.

Phase three: caring and supporting

This phase embraces both the formal and informal means of meeting the needs of people where they are, and the availability of people and resources in times of tragedy, pain and uncertainty.

Prayer ministry – small teams on Sundays and during the week

Some churches have prayer at the front of the church following a service, others have places allocated for prayer. Those praying are typically trained for the ministry, according to the theological approach of the church and what they look for and expect God to do.

Pastoral visitation – organised visits for those with particular needs

We have looked already at the pastoral visit. The visit can be requested by the person or someone close to them.

Pastoral counselling – non-professional and professional

Care may include what might be called 'counselling': one-to-one conversations about what may be holding someone back from experiencing life in all its fullness. Sometimes people prefer to see a counsellor outside their church, as they don't want to share secrets with someone who they see regularly. (CWR has a network of trained counsellors. You can search for your nearest one by visiting waverleyabbeycollege.ac.uk/find-a-counsellor-map)

Emergency pastoral care – crisis care team

In addition to those who regularly provide care, an emergency pastoral care team is brought together at times of crisis. These teams could be the first to respond to a community crisis, such as severe weather, or a crisis affecting a family such as sudden bereavement or bad news.

Welfare and practical care – financial, food and practical ministry teams

These teams might be involved in providing help with people's gardens, providing short-term financial aid if the main earner in a family loses their job, or decorating and refurbishing the home of someone in need.

Healing ministry teams

Healing teams may operate at church services alongside the prayer team; they may be part of a 'Healing on the Street' team, which goes beyond the walls of the church; or they may connect with the church leadership when the sick invite them to anoint with oil.

Neighbourhood leaders / clergy network

These groups specifically help to care for the carers and full-time staff. They are typically a regular gathering of local church leaders who can be intimate enough for real connection but broad enough to include many churches. They facilitate sharing of news and focus as well as a degree of pastoral support. Most leaders would typically have other ways of receiving support in addition.

Mentoring / coaching / spiritual direction – one to one pastoral care

Mentor is the name given to a wise or trusted advisor or guide – a person who is prepared to commit time, experience and skills to help another person grow as an individual in a way that is accepting, caring and beneficial. A mentor is usually more experienced in the faith than the mentoree.

The mentor may focus on an area of growth, a skill that the mentor is experienced in, such as worship leading, or provide ongoing relationship of regular contact where topics are discussed as they come up.

Coaching can be defined as one person facilitating another person's growth in godliness. It uses non-directive questioning to help the person being coached to take action. In coaching, the coach doesn't necessarily have expertise in the topic discussed, but seeks to help the coachee resolve issues themselves.

Spiritual directors are also known as 'soul friends' or 'spiritual friends'. They seek to help Christians discern what God is doing in their life, uncover blockages and make progress in the things that matter. The use of spiritual directors has become common across all denominations and traditions.

Phase four: equipping and training

In this phase, we consider the importance of equipping people to be followers of Jesus because if someone's only connection with the church is to receive care, then they are missing out on all God has for them.

Some ways to equip people might include:

Group discipleship or membership courses
Discipleship is a lifelong process, but that's not to say that a group helping those who are just starting out as disciples isn't a valuable thing. This can include unpacking the basics of the Christian faith, how to pray, how to read the Bible, how to share faith, and what

the Bible says about relationships, time and finances. The small group dimension enables new believers to connect with those at a similar stage of faith to them. Once a discipleship course has been completed, new believers may want to join another small group so that their growth in faith may continue.

Training for those participating in church services

Most churches involve 'lay' people in a whole host of ways within the church service: worship leading, public prayer, personal prayer, Bible reading, welcoming and stewarding. Each of these areas could valuably have training – whether one evening or a series of evenings.

Discovering spiritual gifts

Each Christian has spiritual gifts and can be open to other spiritual gifts that God gives. An evening or a series of evenings where spiritual gifts are defined and discussed with a view to personal discovery can be life changing.

Pastoral leadership training

There are a number of courses that can help people in pastoral oversight including the Growing Leaders course (visit cpas.org.uk for more details).

Pastoral care training

CWR delivers training courses that look at aspects of pastoral care for people who are carers or anticipating undertaking a caring role. Pastoral care can be solitary and energy sapping; training that refreshes or builds on skills in the company of other people can be enormously valuable.

Counselling training

CWR also offers various counselling courses that help people understand how humans are designed to function and how to provide help on a one-to-one basis.

Family and parenting courses

Bringing up a family is a challenge, especially if your own experience was not a good one when you were growing up. I know folk whose parenting has been transformed by regular meetings looking at some of the key issues.

Pre-marriage classes

I had a pastor friend who refused to marry anyone unless he had five sessions with them going through the basics of marriage. My wife and I spent a valuable weekend with a couple who took us through our expectations ahead of married life.

Marriage enrichment sessions

All marriages could benefit from a regular check-up. Sessions that help couples stay on track can be vital.

Healing ministry training

Praying for healing can be very simple, but also fraught with challenge. Is there a correct way? Why aren't more people healed? What about laying on hands? Are some more gifted than others?

Training can enable such questions to be discussed and a consensus reached on what can be said.

Evangelism and outreach training

Many Christians struggle to share their faith and indeed to know what to say when enquiries are raised. Training can be in personal faith, door to door, open air work, and apologetics.

Children and youth ministry training
Wise practice regarding young people in church needs discussing. How is discipline (and fun!) maintained in a church environment? What makes a good session for children and young people? What kind of curriculum is needed?

Small group leaders training
There are many ways to train leaders and much to discuss to enable a small group to thrive. (Again my book *Small Group Essentials* may be useful.)

Sunday teaching series
We have noted that a key part of teaching and equipping comes from the pulpit. Messages may be designed for a number of ends, especially if non-believers are present. But most churches encourage their leadership to teach God's Word so that people are changed as they hear and respond to it.

Web resources
There are plenty of free materials and resources online, but not all of them are good and some are positively harmful – even those with a Christian label. Suggesting appropriate sermons and training material helps equip people who are unable to attend because of other commitments. And if you judiciously select material that is helpful, you can resource your church in countless ways.

Relationship courses

Many churches have struggled to resolve conflict, resulting in ongoing tensions or even a church split. Courses that help people understand a biblical approach can save an awful lot of grief.

Lifestyle courses (eg finances, unemployment)

Around half of Jesus' parables mention or focus on money. We are wise to have a correct attitude: celebrating its blessings and confronting its ills. In particular, helping those out of work to stay buoyant as they seek employment.

Phase five: releasing and facilitating ministry

This phase requires a particular perspective of ministry that may not be always understood.

The fundamental understanding is that everyone is indwelt with the Spirit and therefore capable of ministering, and that this ministry is inside and outside of the local church. In other words, the church does not 'keep' people within its walls and insist that they pour their energy into their part of God's work. Our role is to encourage people to become followers of Jesus and work out what this means in their context. Many will, of course, find that their ministry is in their church, but not everyone will. If we make it clear that we are happy to support people whatever church they attend, they will know that they are cared for personally and not just as a 'number'.

Serving opportunities within the context of the local church

All that said, many of us will want to help people to serve in their local church and part of the leadership's role is to discover what areas might be suitable, or indeed create areas that would work with the gifting they have.

I am always an advocate of giving people appropriate opportunity to serve but within certain constraints. This is not like marriage where you need a degree of certainty before committing. It's quite legitimate to try something out, see how you feel and how God equips you and get feedback from wise leaders. For example, help can be given if you are new to the area of preaching; sermon scripts can be checked and tips given on how to be a competent communicator. Few of us are complete naturals and opportunities may be coupled with appropriate training.

Evangelism and outreach

We have noted that we need to train people in aspects of sharing faith, but it's also important to release people into appropriate avenues of outreach. If they are not a preacher, they may be great chatting one on one; if they are not comfortable with street evangelism, they might be great at leading an evangelistic Bible study. They may have a passion for sport, music or art, which can be avenues through which they make connections and form relationships.

Hospitality

Jesus often taught around the meal table. Releasing people into hospitality ministry is to create potential moments for all manner of interactions.

Short-term and regular ministry teams

Concentrated periods of activity can kick start people's faith and help them realise what their gifting is. Such teams might involve supporting a local church in a period of outreach or children's holiday club. In addition, I have known churches that seek to minister via clearing up the neighbourhood, tidying gardens or putting on sports training camps.

Overseas short-term ministry teams

Teams travel overseas to provide short-term relief, build homes, help with local village work or support evangelistic efforts. Many have returned from these mission trips enthusiastic and fired up in their faith.

Discipleship and mentoring

It's easy to recommend discipleship and mentoring in a book, but perhaps harder to find people to be involved. Many serious believers could simply offer to mentor younger believers. There is more advice on mentoring in my book, *Coaching and Mentoring*[3].

Specialist ministries – using gifts and expertise to help others

It's quite possible that the Christians we seek to help 'into ministry' may already be engaged in ministry through their job or leisure activity and that we need to simply facilitate them to utilise their expertise in a church setting. We would not seek to undermine their professional work of course, but simply give them an outlet that blesses them and those they serve.

Local community ministries

There will be areas of ministry locally that need support: charitable activities, school ministries and ministry to the elderly.

Business, commercial and industrial ministries – ministry in the workplace

Many still operate as if God is only interested in what is done in the local church and has no interest in the rest of life. However, the Bible says: 'whatever you do, whether in word or deed, do it all in the name of the Lord Jesus, giving thanks to God the Father through him' (Col. 3:17). Supporting people, prayerfully and communally, in their workplace might be to encourage them to see that their job has been 'their ministry' all along: they just haven't seen it that way.

Having looked at these five phases, it's worth now reflecting that church life is rarely this smooth.

Not everyone enters church one Sunday, get connected three weeks later, raise their needs of care after six weeks, become equipped after three months and then released into ministry after six months.

People are at various stages of faith, and have levels of connection already. They may be well connected to Christians before they ever enter church. Or have a ministry from a previous church, which they could utilise almost from day one, though the church leadership will probably want to get to know them a bit first. And those engaged in ministry may need pastoral care too.

So it's more important to ensure that all phases are catered for and to consider what phase people may be at, than it is to expect newcomers to travel through each phase.

Questions to consider

• Looking at the five phases, as a church, which is your strongest area? Which is your weakest area?

_____

_____

• Are there simple things you can do now as a result of reading this chapter?

_____

_____

• What things will you need to talk with others about?

_____

_____

• What things may take a few months to implement?

_____

_____

• Draw a diagram charting your flow from newcomer through to participating in ministry. What does this tell you, if anything?

_____

_____

[1]Chip and Dan Heath, *Made to Stick* (New York, USA: Random House, 2007)
[2]Andy Peck, *Small Group Essentials* (Farnham: CWR, 2017)
[3]Andy Peck, *Coaching and Mentoring* (Farnham: CWR, 2015)

10: Care for those on the fringe

It's often thought that the quality of the first team in a club sport is the key element for success. Certainly it's these players who make the headlines, attract the fans and determine the outcome of the trophies. But an undervalued part of any team are the players who don't play regularly, sometimes known as the 'fringe players'. It's important that these people are motivated, strong and fit, so that they are ready to play well if called upon. Sometimes major fringe players have become instrumental in teams winning trophies much to everyone's surprise.

Most churches have a number of fringe people. They are not 'fringe' because they can't get a game! Thankfully, in the local church, everyone gets to take part. You don't get a text on Saturday night informing you that your presence is not required! They are 'fringe' because they are a) on the way in to the church, b) on their way out or c) happy to remain on the fringe, however that is understood.

Being on the fringe does not necessarily mean people are moving away from God. Our purpose here is how to extend love to those in need at the fringe of the church, believing that being on the fringe could be less than ideal for them and the rest of the church.

First we need to look at each of the three categories – on the way in, on the way out and on the fringe – before looking at how we may care for each.

Those on the way in

We have already seen the importance of establishing a good way for newcomers to become connected. Those on the way in may be on the fringe because they have not been assisted correctly with the information and relationships required to move them into the heart of the church. Many of the challenges that we find being part of any group can be the same in the local church. We can feel excluded because of: race, class, perceptions that we are not like others in the group, sexual orientation, income, dress code, language and being unfamiliar with the rules.

Inevitably, the culture of the people in any given locality will determine the feel of the church. But let's be clear that nothing should exclude people from hearing the gospel, and every church needs to make sure that they are not creating barriers about things that do not reside in the gospel. The apostle Paul said: 'I have become all things to all people so that by all possible means I might save some' (1 Cor. 9:22), meaning that, without committing a sin, Paul adapted his behaviour in order to remove any barriers, which might prevent others listening to his preaching.

In the long run, relationships will speak louder than the best worship service or preaching. Feeling isolated or on the edge when you want to belong is quite uncomfortable – possibly painful. If we have a few good friends in a local church, we will usually be able to weather most church crises, but if we don't, almost anything might drag us away.

We noted in the last chapter that entry points to the church family must be clear and accessible for a new person. Churches that are only friendly with the 'in crowd' are not always aware of how hard it is for a new person to break into the life of the congregation.

Those who are new followers of Jesus will discover many unfamiliar things if they come into a local congregation. Here are a few of those things:

- The style of meeting
- The music
- The Bible
- What we do in the meeting (service)
- The language used
- The church culture, including expectations and taboos
- The people

Let's remember how marginalised the Church has become in society over recent years. There is no longer a presumption of faith. The percentage of the population who call themselves Christians is at the lowest level ever with many people in the 18–30s bracket saying they have no faith at all. The media no longer typically respect the Christian line on moral issues, with Christian MPs facing strong criticism if their view deviates from the popular humanist perspective.

Well-publicised moral failures of well-known church leaders and media exposure of what we are against (rather than for) has pushed Christianity in wider western society into a place of distrust, which has to be overcome through positive relationship experiences before people are willing to consider our point of view.

Some of those on the way in will be people moving from another church. These can be for positive reasons or reasons of necessity, such as relocating for work or retirement. Some move churches because of painful experiences. The important thing is to hear their story sympathetically, but remember there is always at least two points of view in any conflict situation. Encourage the newcomers to bring closure to their previous hurtful experiences wherever possible. If the emotional damage remains unaddressed it may interfere with their ability to move on and integrate in the new church. If necessary, provide help to facilitate conversations with anyone they have fallen out with. Be a listener. You may need to be a mediator but avoid being an arbitrator or judge. These people may not be in a position to trust a church again in the short term. Your church may be a half-way place to their final destination.

Pastoring people on the way in

It's generally wise to give people a good length of time to settle in before involving them in public ministry. They need to know for sure that this is the church they want to be part of, and to know enough about the ethos of the church, so that they can feel comfortable being involved and supporting its leadership.

Where possible it is good practice to check that all is well with the church they have previously attended. This needs to be with the full consent of the newcomer. Newcomers may be reluctant to blow their own trumpet if they have gifts that can be utilised. Equally a church leader may have cause to make some helpful comments that will ensure they settle in smoothly and well.

If it's clear that someone has been coming for say six months but is still merely attending a service and not engaging in anything more, it may be worth checking that they know what's on and what they can get involved in. It's surprising how unaware people can be of things that may seem basic to regular attenders. Some people might require a little gentle coaxing for them to connect better. I would stress the importance of not coming across as 'needing' their involvement. Deepening church connections are for mutual benefit and this is not to make any judgment about the time they are taking. But it does mean that precious time is not wasted if they merely need a gentle nudge.

Those on the way out

There is very little hard evidence for why people leave a church, though we might be able to guess the reasons.

In their books, *Gone but not Forgotten*[1] and *Gone for Good?*[2], Leslie Francis and Philip Richter asked church-leavers why they left. Alan Jamieson wrote the book, *Churchless Faith*[3] in 2000 based on conversations with believers (or former believers) in New Zealand, and more recently, in 2016, Steve Aisthorpe wrote *The Invisible Church*[4] based on his research in the islands off the north coast of Scotland.

These books give us some hard data on why people say they leave:
• Changes in belief and unbelief
• Major life changes and transitions
• Alternative lives and alternative meanings
• Lifestyles incompatible with church membership
• Not belonging or fitting in
• Costs of churchgoing outweighing benefits
• Disillusionment with the church
• Seeming irrelevance of the church

- Problems with change
- Problems with forms of worship
- Leadership problems
- Church seeming too liberal

Loss of faith

In Francis and Richter's *Gone for Good?*, it states that one in three church-leavers pointed to loss of faith as his or her key reason for leaving. Loss of faith was a key for men, younger people and for Roman Catholics. Loss of faith has become a less of a factor in recent years. Those who leave through loss of faith are unlikely to come back.

Incompatible lifestyles

Again, Francis and Richter found that one fifth of church-leavers said that they left because aspects of their lifestyle seemed unacceptable to the church. Such issues were significant for men, for those under the age of 40, and for Roman Catholics. Those who leave for this reason are unlikely to come back.

Working hours

Conflicts with the demands of work, especially Sunday working, influenced one in four church-leavers. This is a factor of equal significance among men and women, across the age groups, and across the denominations. Pressure of work has become a more important factor in recent years. Those who leave due to the pressure of work are quite likely to return when the time is right.

Problems with change

One in every five church-leavers disengaged after experiencing problems with change in the church. New hymns, new service books, new translations of the Bible and new styles of worship all contributed challenges and obstacles to churchgoers who were uncomfortable with change. Even the arrival of a new minister brought with it the problem of change. Problems with change were particularly salient for older church-leavers and Anglicans. Those who leave citing change as the reason are among those who may seek opportunities to come back.

Steve Aisthorpe reported that a number of people said that leaving a particular church enabled them to follow Jesus better: they regarded the church as injurious to their following of Jesus. They claimed to still read the Bible, pray and share their faith and receive their spiritual nourishment from conferences, podcasts and meeting with likeminded friends from time to time.

Pastoring those on the way out

If someone is on the fringe because they are intending to leave, what can we do?

1. We can help them to reconcile with fellow believers. Even if they do leave, it cannot be good for anyone to have unresolved issues and continuing personal pain. If it is an issue with the leadership, then space needs to be sought so that they can understand the ministers' point of view. In some cases, it may be a case of 'agreeing to differ' but clearly there will be issues where certain opinions are regarded as spiritually unhealthy and leaders are wise to lovingly warn them of the consequences.

2. In some cases, people require a safe place to share and discuss faith doubts. If they have unthinkingly embraced a childhood faith that they have never thought through, it can be a helpful time to re-work their faith in the light of new reading of Scripture or

consideration of challenging issues. In churches where it's 'the party line or nothing', little room is given for any dissenting voice and certainly no space for discussion, which is badly needed.

3. If someone is on the fringe because of lifestyle issues, then they will need to be loved and prayed for and encouraged to know God's love and grace. It doesn't mean we approve of what is happening but we remember that God is the judge, not us. The Pharisees excluded people on behaviour, Jesus was always concerned with the heart, and we should be too. Our aim and goal is to help people walk wisely. In extreme cases, we may have to step in as Matthew recommends: 'If your brother or sister sins, go and point out their fault, just between the two of you' (Matt. 18:15). Only as a last resort, and in very extreme cases, might it be necessary to exclude them – but we hope and pray it never comes to that.

4. Sadly, some churches have failed to model and exhibit the grace and goodness of God, and perhaps it's no surprise that people feel they need to move on. I would always counsel people to work at praying that things may change before they leave, for God may have brought them to the church for the purpose of restoring the body. The image that may help is the man who stands on a large block of ice. If their personal warmth melts the ice, then all is well. What is concerning is when the block of ice freezes the man. Each person needs to decide whether it is spiritually injurious to stay.

5. Why not contact people who have left your church and see how they are doing? If appropriate, and if you have the right kind of relationship with them, ask them why they have left, and what you can learn as a church from their departure. You may regard their reason for leaving as personal, or it may be that their comment sheds light on your activities that can be of help to others.

Those who prefer to remain on the fringe

For some churches, being on the fringe is an OK place for people to be. The church is large and no one may actually know how many are part of the church, and how many are on the fringe. The belief is that those who want to become better connected have ample opportunity and it's up to them to be as close or distant as they want. This is especially prevalent within larger city churches of all denominations.

The traditional understanding of the faith journey is that belief comes before behaviour and then you belong: believe, behave, belong. But increasingly churches are discovering that we need to help people belong before they can believe and then behave.

Some people may prefer to stay on the fringe: they have a faith and want to come to the church but have no intention of getting more involved. This may be because they want to pursue a lifestyle that they feel would be frowned upon, or have perhaps been overwhelmed by being too much involved either at this church or another.

Many other churches encourage or strongly push for engagement by those who attend. 'You are a school teacher, are you? Good! We need help with our kids programme.' In these churches, you would be hard pressed to stay on the fringe and have to work hard at avoiding the church's entreaties for help!

Some people remain on the fringe of the church because they have actually decided that they are not willing to pay the price to be part of the inner core of the church. It may be that they would 'theoretically' want to be more involved, but have decided that they don't want to make the changes they think they would need to make.

Others are on the fringe of the church because they occasionally come to church activities, use the church building or have family members who do. Many have no apparent intention of becoming Christians or getting more involved.

How well the church addresses its fringe will depend to a large extent on which way it faces as a unit. Does it tend to face inward and look after, primarily, the 'flock', or does it look both inward and outward? Family atmosphere is good. But a good family seeks to widen, rather than narrow. I have come across stories of people who found the actual attendance of a church service very intimidating; people who got as far as the church door a number of times before having the courage to enter the building; a woman who assumed she couldn't bring her husband because he wasn't a 'member'.

Many people on the fringe of a church are likely to find the experience of congregational life to be outside their comprehension and perhaps their comfort zone. The discomfort can arise from a number of reasons. Here are a few:

• Not understanding the jargon or elements of the church service.
• Feeling different or ignorant about things that members of the church took for granted.
• Not understanding 'in jokes'.
• Feeling awkward when money is requested.
• Unfamiliar format – sitting for long periods, singing, listening to a talk is not what they do in daily life.
• Seemingly dated way of doing church.

While it still has its place in some situations, people learn differently now and experience life through different channels.

One church chose to have a 'cigarette break' to help newcomers feel comfortable. They weren't advocating smoking, just recognising that the attenders who smoked might feel more comfortable and concentrate better if that facility was open to them.

Pastoring those who prefer to remain on the fringe

Our primary concern for anyone is that they come to know Christ and grow in Him. To that end, it's good to do all we can to encourage people to move in a Christward direction. Fringe dwellers need love, grace, understanding and the work of the Spirit of God to help them in that movement. That must be our prayerful activity.

It can take a considerable time before someone feels comfortable enough to even want to be more involved. Many have so little experience of church and the Bible that the culture shift is massive and we are wise to not expect too much too soon. Many of us became warm to the gospel and church over many months or years, and we are wise to remember that their journey will be similar.

There is no 'one size fits all' strategy that can move people on in a godly direction, hence the importance of creating opportunities for real communication so that issues can be dealt with that may help their faith journey.

Ultimately, our job is not to try to force anyone to become more involved or to stop them leaving. Jesus invited all to come to Him and never turned anyone away but people excluded themselves as they discovered what He required. As people in the church display the benefits of walking with Christ and know an infectious joy in Him, the hope is that people will also want to become true and faithful disciples.

Questions to consider

• Which category of people is largest in your church: those on their way in, those on the fringe, or those on their way out (as best you can guess!)?

• Are there simple things you can do immediately that could show care for any of these people?

• What would you expect from a regular church member in terms of attendance and involvement?

[1] Leslie Francis and Philip Richter, *Gone but not Forgotten* (London: Darton, Longman & Todd, 1998)
[2] Leslie Francis and Philip Richter, *Gone for Good? Church leaving and returning in the twenty-first century* (London: Epworth Press, 2007)
[3] Alan Jamieson, *Churchless Faith: Faith journeys beyond the churches* (London: SPCK, 2000)
[4] Steve Aisthorpe, *The Invisible Church* (Norwich: St Andrew's Press, 2016)

 # 11: Expand care beyond the church

We have seen in this book that care flows from our walk with Christ and desire to live as He lived. It's clear that part of Jesus' ministry was the training and equipping of the Twelve. In that sense, He had a special group to whom He gave particular attention and care. But His invitation for all people to follow Him implies that no one is actually excluded from care; for example, there is no record of anyone being refused healing. (We noted earlier in the book that the delay to Lazarus was the purpose of raising him from the dead, and the Syro-Phonecian woman had her need met after some curious light-hearted banter with Jesus.)

His indiscriminate love and care for all who came to Him was the model for all who would seek to learn what He taught. Jesus does not vet anyone. He is the standard for inclusivity! His audience was typically people who might count themselves as being part of the covenant God had made with Israel. But there were manifestly many who were regarded as 'sinners' (and outside the community), who had for all practical purposes given up on religion – especially the religion of the Pharisees, whose additional rules and regulations had left them bemused and bewildered. Jesus cares for people's physical need, always aware that their deeper need is their relationship with God.

In general, churches focus their pastoral care resources upon those who are already part of the church. There is wisdom in this. We have the injunction: 'Therefore, as we have opportunity, let us do good to all people, especially to those who belong to the family of believers' (Gal. 6:10).

We have seen that pastoring in the biblical sense involves shepherding the flock, which by definition will be those who follow the good shepherd. And those outside the church community are not always willing to be helped by people with a church connection, especially if they fear that they will be preached at.

Typically, more time and energy is devoted to the pastoral needs within a church than evangelism (the sharing of the good news with non-believers). But, like so many debates, it is not a case of either/or but both/and. Furthermore, the suggestion that we can always distinguish between the two is not always accurate.

I was intrigued by the words of Glen Scrivener, evangelist and director of the ministry Speak Life:

'"What must I do to be saved?" Every evangelist is prepared for the question. Few are asked it. Still, we're ready. We've polished our rifles, loaded our silver bullets, and lain in wait to ambush our unsuspecting prey. The minute they fall into our trap we'll let 'em have it, right between the eyes.

It rarely occurs to us that the battle is actually being fought with different weapons, on another hill, in a distant country. The questions people are asking are more like this: What's wrong with me? What's wrong with my family? How can I overcome these fears? Why can't I get my act together? How do I handle a bullying boss?

And the list goes on. This is where the battle rages and where our evangelism must engage.

Unfortunately, we miss these opportunities, largely because we've divided our forces. We recruit the hard-headed for evangelism and send them to (what we imagine to be) the front lines. We recruit the soft-hearted for pastoral care and put them in the field hospital.

While such a divide seems natural to us, it's alien to the Bible.

In the Bible evangelists are bringers of good news, given by God to build up the church (Eph. 4:11). Pastors (shepherds) are hardy fighters who battle wolves and save the lost (Acts 20:28–29; Luke 15:6). Evangelists and pastors are far more similar than we usually believe. Both are ministers of the Word, applying the same gospel to the same set of human problems.'[1]

Scrivener helpfully reminds us that sharing faith and caring for people should be a part of the same ministry. We might suggest that what Jesus brought together let not man separate...!

The Church as a whole has also debated the importance of caring for people's physical needs over their spiritual. Classic Bible believing churches have underplayed the need to care for the whole person, knowing that saving people's souls is the priority. Churches that have majored on physical care believe those focusing on the soul lack compassion. In some countries, the perceived difference is also connected to political beliefs with those more conservative politically concerned for the soul and the more liberal caring for the whole person.

Both sides can find biblical support, which suggests that the issue is not cut and dried. But consider this: in the Old Testament the word *mishpat* is used to describe the importance of treating people equitably. It includes fair acquittal or punishment based on the evidence of a person's case. However, *mishpat* also involves giving a person their rights. This includes protection and care, and this should be focused on care of the 'poor and needy' (Deut. 15:11) and the 'orphans and widows' (James 1:27). So when Jesus calls us to seek first the kingdom of God and His righteousness, the word 'justice' could have been transposed instead of righteousness. If Christians ignore justice they ignore something that God is concerned for.

However, let's be absolutely clear that, as we have said throughout this book, we should long that everyone knows God personally. As we care for the body, we need to talk about the soul and care in the name of the one who loved us and gave Himself for us. Too many churches exercise glorified social work, and take comfort in the large numbers they care for, even though they perhaps rarely engage in faith conversations. They are like the man who hands a hungry child a sandwich but fails to tell him that the building is on fire.

Our motivation is key. In the name of Christ, we seek to love all who God brings across our path by meeting the presenting need. As the old saying goes: 'They don't care how much you know, they just want to know how much you care.' Our care is not some kind of 'trick' to get them to like us and embrace our faith. Pastoral care is not an evangelistic strategy but it will involve looking for opportunities to share the fact that God loves them – He is our chief delight.

How do we expand care beyond the congregation?

Involving every member
We have been saying that pastoral care is expressing love for people in need so that they may find, deepen and develop their faith in Jesus. This opportunity exists for everyone from every church.

Care can be easily expanded beyond the walls of the church if the people who make up the church realise they are 'church' where they are. The church exists (in one sense) wherever its people are. If they are prayerfully aiming to follow Jesus then it will be no surprise if they find themselves connecting with people and caring for them appropriately as opportunity arises. It's the friendship connections that may lead to an opportunity to provide particular care when the need becomes apparent. Of course, these may be geographically a long way from where the gathered church typically meets; work, leisure and family connections take members to minister to people who may never attend a church.

The work and ministry of Bill Hybels, former senior pastor of Willow Creek Community Church, Chicago has helped me in this regard. He used a formula to outline what he believed to be the key elements in someone specifically sharing their faith with others and the formula works equally well as we broaden this to focus on pastoral care. The formula is: C.C. + V.W. + H.P. = M.I. (C.C. Close connection; V.W. Verbal witness; H.P. High potency and M.I. Maximum impact).[2]

Hybels believes that for us to have maximum impact in our personal witness, we need to have close connection with non-believers and share something of our faith journey with them, but also be sufficiently close to the Lord ourselves (he calls this 'high potency') that our life speaks of God's love.

Hybels explains that if any of these ingredients are missing, not much happens. We can be highly potent (on fire for God) and ready to share but not closely connected. We can be closely connected and sharing our faith, but not walking closely with God. And we can be closely connected and highly potent, but not say anything to them about our faith!

We have seen that caring as Jesus did means caring for the whole person, including exploring how they are with God. But even if verbal witness is off the table, in order to truly care for people, we need to be connected to them first. It is possible, of course, to care for a stranger in a workplace, sport or leisure situation where a shared interest creates a connection and we learn of need. But we all know that people typically go to people they know and are more open to receiving care from people they know.

All of this raises the question: do church members have sufficient connection with people outside the church community? If most of the people are spending time 'running the show' (the church) then there will be little opportunity to be anything other than inward looking.

Studies show that within three years of coming to faith, most new Christians have no non-Christian friends. (This can be for a combination of reasons of course: some new believers feel they need to leave friendships that they perceive might harm their walk with Christ and equally some non-believers drop their newly converted friend.) It's no surprise that when the church puts on an outreach event or runs a seekers' course such as Alpha, many church members struggle to find non-believing friends to invite.

Thus, the starting point of equipping believers to care is to find opportunities in services, small groups and special training events to talk through issues surrounding making time for people and sharing the Christian faith in a non-cheesy and relaxed way. At CWR, I run courses on sharing Jesus and explain to attendees that you need to hear 'their story' before you share anything. What has been their journey with God, church and faith, if at all? Until that is understood, you won't know what is appropriate. You can then reflect whether anything of 'your story' of knowing God could be mentioned. Finally, there is 'God's story: the gospel', which you can share, but in ways that fit their likely level of understanding. The Holy Spirit can guide you as to which 'story' may be most appropriate in any situation. It's not rocket science and it can be the most natural thing in the world.

Michael Harvey, founder of Unlocking the Growth and co-founder of Back to Church Sunday, said that, in his experience, 70% of church members could name someone who God has placed on their heart to invite to church. But when asked the follow up question: 'Do you intend to invite them?' Just 5–15% said, 'Yes'. The number one reason for not inviting was fear. Somehow, we need to care enough to overcome fear and nervousness to interact with people, whether we invite them to church or not.

Know your local church neighbourhood

Having worked to enable the local church to be engaged in caring for those they come across, we next think of the area the church serves. Many churches do not especially operate within a defined boundary. City centre churches draw people from across the city where speedy communications enable people to choose the church that ticks their social and spiritual boxes. But most local churches will have an idea of who they are seeking to reach and for a good proportion this would be via an understanding of our 'neighbourhood' or the general area from which people come to the gathering. We can pick up what goes on just by walking around the area but often the actual details of the area are hidden from us.

On the UK Office for National Statistic's w~' (nomisweb.co.uk), you can type the postcode ~~ in the box marked, 'Local area report' and statistics of your ward, parish and local a useful tool for understanding the area and for getting answers to questions such as:

1. What sort of age range is there?

You will need to know the specific demography for your situation together with statistics and insight on single parents, major employers, homelessness, poverty, wealth and local recent history or tensions.

If you have many young families in the neighbourhood, what are their particular needs? If the elderly predominate, how can you minister to them?

2. What is the religious make up?

According to the 2011 census, 59% of the UK population identify as Christian, 25% would describe themselves as having no religion, 7% have a religion but don't state what, 4.8% are Muslim, 1.5% Hindu, 0.8% Sikh, 0.5% Jewish and 0.4% Buddhist.

If a particular religion is represented in your area, how well do you know what they believe? If someone from that religion comes to faith in Jesus, what might that mean? Do you know the leaders of these religions locally? How might you reach out to them, especially in times when local feeling may not be particularly positive?

3. How is your neighbourhood (area) distinct from the town/ city/rural community in which you are located?

The Office for National Statistics included this comment:

'While the population as a whole is ageing and growth in numbers is greatest in the south and east, Census 2011 shows that local ommunities, often only a short journey apart, have dramatically different experiences, lifestyles and identities. Correspondingly different demands are made on governments, neighbours and families for health care, work, housing and other services.'

I recall chatting with a church planter in Brighton who was intending to plant a church in Moulsecoomb, even though they already had a small church in that area. Although close to one another in the north of Brighton, the planter knew that the people of Moulsecoomb would be unlikely to attend their church because of perceived distinctions in the area by locals.

4. What is the size of households?

If you have a higher percentage of people living on their own, how might this affect the kind of events you offer? People living on their own may be more prone to loneliness.

Co-habiting will be high nationwide. Many newcomers may well be co-habiting as a couple. Of course, most churches would not regard this as ideal, but when the culture moves, the church will need to be firm in what it believes but aware of the journey that attendees might be on and give them space to start that journey.

5. What about immigration?

In 2017, about 86% of the UK population were born in the UK and about 90% were British nationals compared with about 89% and 93% respectively in 2007 (according to UK National Statistics, ons.gov.uk).

Do you have a ministry to immigrants? What are their needs? How easily can they be assimilated into your church?

6. What about debt levels?

British households spent around £900 more on average than they received in income during 2017, meaning their finances went into deficit for the first time since the credit boom of the 1980s.

What is your policy on offering financial help? Do you offer any debt prevention advice? How often is debt looked at in church meetings?

7. What is church attendance like?

Some key findings from the Church Statistics report are:

'UK Church membership has declined from 10.6 million in 1930 to 5.5 million in 2010, or as a percentage of the population; from about 30% to 11.2%. By 2013, this had declined further to 5.4 million (10.3%). If current trends continue, membership will fall to 8.4% of the population by 2025.'

Church membership is declining in all four constituent countries of the UK, but in England the decline is relatively small, whereas the biggest decline appears to be in Scotland.

'In 1950, 67% of all babies in England were baptised in the Church of England. In the 1990s, three out of ten newborns have been baptised. In the Church of England, the decline in terms of Sunday attendances is about 1% per year. Only about 2% of the population is now in an Anglican church on any given Sunday (with 10% plus in church overall).'

If this rate continues, by 2020 the vast majority of 25 year olds are unlikely to feel any personal attachment to the Church of England. Such statistics can be seen as depressing. They are repeated here because it gives us perspective on how things are and if you are finding it tough, that is not surprising.

However, many people are still identifying themselves as 'Christian' (72% of them according to an Independent Television Commission survey) and there are churches that are growing and vibrant in this very same environment, so let's be inspired to explore ways to expand our pastoral care.

Acting on what you know

Once you have worked on your research, the next step is to prayerfully consider what to do with the information.

• What feasible ways could you care for the needs of the community?
• Is there anyone who might be able to head that up? Is there any indication that God is already stirring people to act?
• Are there things you already do, which could be adapted to meet some of the needs you have?
• Do you have people within the church who are facing needs, which could be expanded to outside the church?
• What kind of resources are required: people, money, time?
• What would be the lead time for any new venture?
• Can you test a new venture in a small way to see if it has any interest?

Ministries

If you are looking for inspiration regarding ministry options, here's some ways that churches and charities have responded to what they perceive as their need.

• Debt counselling – John Kirkby started Christians Against Poverty in 1996, looking to use his experience in finance to help the poor. Today, there are over 600 debt centres that help churches do a range of activities surrounding debt.

- Dementia clubs – some churches have opened memory cafés to cater for older people who have dementia, and their carers.
- Toddler clubs – many churches provide opportunities for parents and carers to gather.
- Soup kitchens – provision of hot meals for those who are on low income and/or homeless.
- Addiction recovery courses – provides support for those recovering from a range of addictions.
- Recovery from divorce – an opportunity for folk who have gone through break up to share together.
- Parenting courses – these are often DVD-led courses that provide advice on raising children.
- Pre-marriage course – engaged couples learn what marriage is about and how to navigate tensions.
- Marriage courses – married couples reflect on their marriage and possible areas for improvement.
- Homework clubs – many local churches liaise with local schools to help provide a safe place for children between end of school and parents' return from work.
- Counselling and coaching – some churches provide counselling and coaching free of charge for a fixed period.
- Mentoring youth – mentoring schemes to help young people, particularly those with absent fathers.
- Job clubs – these groups provide regular support for job seekers and help with CVs and interviews.
- Supporting asylum seekers – the charity Upbeat Communities has considerable experience and is open to assisting other

churches interested in starting a ministry in this area
(visit upbeatcommunities.org for more details).

• Youth on the streets – the Nicodemus Trust aims to help young
people living on the streets and is keen to help local churches
who wish to start a ministry.

• Helping ex-offenders – there is a network connected with Alpha
in Prisons that helps rehabilitate former offenders in connection
with The Prison Fellowship.

• Healing on the streets – this ministry began at Causeway
Vineyard Church, Coleraine and provides training for churches
that wish to set up a ministry in their locality.

• Furnishing a house – one church developed a ministry of
recycling and refurbishing furniture so it was available for
people unable to afford to furnish their home.

• Neighbourhood clear up – a dedicated day or weekend tidying
a neighbourhood or dealing with areas not covered by the local
council.

If you are seeking to improve care for your members, you may find
that expanding care beyond your congregation feels like a bridge
too far but as you look outwards, God has a way of taking care of
His people too.

Questions to consider

• Think about the neighbourhood where your church is located.
Are there social aspects that require research?

• If you had more personnel to meet the pastoral needs in the area, what might you do, given your present knowledge of the area?

_____

_____

• What do other churches do in your neighbourhood that you cannot (or will not) do?

_____

_____

• Are there needs beyond the resources of one individual church where joint projects might be more appropriate?

_____

_____

• If you were making a presentation to your church's leadership about this, what would you say?

_____

_____

[1] Glen Scrivener, 'Evangelism and pastoral care: the best of friends', posted 20 July 2017, taken from thegospelcoalition.org [Accessed March 2019]
[2] Bill Hybels, *Just Walk Across the Room* (Grand Rapids, MI, USA: Zondervan, 2006)

12: Develop your vision for pastoral care

We began the book looking at what Jesus preached: a vision of the kingdom of God. He is our chief shepherd and model of how to care. Jesus is Lord of your church and its chief pastor. You can be sure that He has some ideas on what your church can become and how His kind of care can inspire, equip and mobilise you to care for others where He has placed you.

If this book has done its job, vison has already been developing and you are excited about the future. We started the book looking at making incremental gains, and how to up our game. It's time now to put some actions in place for the future.

Vision for change can be grandiose and ethereal but essentially, it is thinking about people we know and what we can do for them. How can we care for folk within our church family and further afield better? As has been famously said: 'nothing becomes dynamic until it becomes specific'. Imagine some specific people in your mind's eye who may need care. Think of some groups of people who aren't yet part of your church family. How can they be connected with, so that they might become followers of Jesus?

The current state of play

It's helpful to evaluate where things are at present. If there are staff who are full time in pastoral care, they are well placed for this evaluation but they may be too close to the ministry to have an objective evaluation, especially if they are mostly responding to crises.

Consider what you know so far:

1. What kind of care do you provide? Consider whether your care is proactive or reactive and to what proportions. Are you typically providing for a particular people group? A particular age group?

2. Who do you currently help?

3. What proportion of people that you help are inside the church and what proportion are outside the church?

4. Are there opportunities as part of your pastoral care to invite people to know God's rule and reign afresh?

5. Think of the ministries of the church. What ages are represented? How are each category cared for?

6. How are care needs made known?

7. How would you evaluate your care? Care evaluation is tricky of course, especially as we look at the concerns of helping people grow as Christians. Many will be pleased with whatever care they receive, regardless. But it's useful to consider whether people are growing as Christians, however you decide to measure it.

8. Have there been problems with care? We must be honest about what is not working and learn from it. Is the problem with the structure (we are missing people)? Is it with the carers (we/they didn't serve well)? Is it with the complexity (we didn't understand what we were doing)?

Future care

How will you develop or adapt your vision for pastoral care? Sometimes it's valuable to have a whole church discussion. In larger churches, you may use a questionnaire. Maybe you could appoint a sub-committee of interested people to report back to the decision making body. Who needs to be involved given the structure of your church? How much time will you give developing a vision?

These things can take time. Don't expect it to happen overnight, but don't let it drag on too long. Remember that it will take time for people to understand and reflect on the changes.

Typically, pastoral care visions are announced in church services. Sometimes a vision document is produced that is circulated. If the church has a members' meeting, that may be the obvious time. By and large, improving pastoral care is unlikely to be controversial, though using additional funds may be, especially if they are taken from something else.

Philosophy

• What is your vision for pastoral care?

_____

_____

_____

• How would you define pastoral care in your context?

_____

_____

• Which of the following areas would you like to be part of your pastoral care?
   – Prayer ministry
   – Pastoral visits
   – Counselling
   – Coaching
   – Mentoring

People

• Who is responsible for pastoral care in your local church or organisation?

_____

_____

• How is your pastoral care evaluated?

_____

_____

• Do you have people in your congregation or known to you who could serve as counsellors?
   – Trained but not accredited
   – Accredited

• How would you form (or expand) a pastoral care team?

_____

• If someone volunteered, how would you respond?

_____

• How well are the carers cared for?

_____

• Is there sufficient supervision?

_____

• Is there sufficient evaluation?

_____

• How good are the pastoral team at taking breaks and help when they need it?

_____

• Is there evidence that some people are over dependent on individuals within the pastoral care team?

_____

Finances

• How are you supporting care financially?

_____

• Which of the following would be part of your budget?
  – Trained counsellors from time to time
  – Trained mentors from time to time
  – Training events
  – Hardship fund
  – Room hire
  – Training courses
  – Refreshments

• How do you handle requests to the church for money?

• How do you handle requests to the church for support with housing or transport?

Areas to consider

Relationships
• Would you marry a couple where either have been divorced?
• Would it depend on why they divorced and whether they were a Christian at the time?
• Do you believe in blessing same-sex couples who are Christians?
• Would you marry a same-sex couple?
• Does the answer to the above depend on whether they are believers or not?
• Do you urge same-sex attracted Christians to be celibate?
• Would you urge couples living together to get married?

• Would you allow someone romantically attached and living with their partner to be involved in Christian ministry in the church?

Family life
• How would you help a couple considering separation and/or divorce?
• Do you have adequate safe-guarding training for all those involved in pastoral care?
• How would you help someone unsure of their sexual identity?

Discipleship issues
• How much should the church leadership be proactive in its care for members in the following areas?
  – Spiritual
  – Physical
  – Mental
  – Social
  – Relational
  – Vocational

• If someone is behaving in ways that do not honour God, what should happen? Does it depend what it is?

The purpose of these questions is to highlight that the best method of intervention or care is not always immediately obvious. But if church leadership discuss matters, it allows the team to do some hard thinking ahead of any crisis.

The advantage of a thought through approach (or policy) is that you are less likely to be swayed in your decision by the personality of the person involved, and in particular their relationship with you.

Next actions

This kind of exercise can overwhelm us and we can end up doing nothing, so it's important to consider what you can do towards improvement and plan other areas later.

• What will you aim to do first?

_____

• We can look for the tricky things when the plain and simple is right in front of us. Are there some easy things you can do and put right?

_____

Think of a time frame for progress.
• What can you do in the next month?

_____

_____

_____

• In the next six months?

_____

_____

_____

• By the next year?

_____

_____

_____

• Are there things you can test out in miniature, which might give
  you an idea on whether they may work more widely?

_____

_____

You would expect this exercise to take some time to complete
and, of course, you will want to involve others as you consider
the questions. But remember that time spent doing this now will
save you time and effort in the long run. As you do it prayerfully
and thoughtfully, be sure that God will be with you in your
consideration. Ask God to expand your vision for all that He can do
in your church and community.

Recommended books

David Allen, *Getting Things Done: The Art of Stress-free Productivity* (London: Piatkus, 2015)

Henry Cloud and John Townsend, *Boundaries* (Grand Rapids, MI, USA: Zondervan, 2004)

Richard Foster, *Celebration of Discipline: The Path to Spiritual Growth* (London: Hodder & Stoughton, 2008)

Selwyn Hughes, *Christ Empowered Living* (Farnham: CWR, 2005)

Ron Kallmier, *Caring and Counselling* (Farnham: CWR, 2012)

Trevor Partridge, *Love with Skin On* (Farnham: CWR, 2016)

Trevor Partridge, *Paraclesis: Coming alongside others* (Farnham: CWR, 2017)

Dallas Willard, *Renovation of the Heart* (London: IVP, 2002)

Dallas Willard, *The Spirit of the Disciplines* (Nashville, TN, USA: HarperOne, 1999)

People helping and pastoral care events, resources and training

People helping is about effectively caring for the people around you. At CWR, we aim to support you in caring for others in their daily lives, workplaces and relationships by providing resources and practical training underpinned by a biblical understanding of emotional and mental health.

CWR Insight Series goes deeper into understanding life's issues and struggles. Drawing on real-life studies, biblical examples and counselling practices, the books and courses offer insight on issues such as depression, anxiety, stress, anger and self-acceptance.

CWR are privileged to partner with Kintsugi Hope, a charity founded by Patrick and Diane Regan in 2018, in offering insight, teaching and support to anyone affected by emotional and mental health issues.

Waverley Abbey College – the educational arm of CWR offers counselling training delivered within a Christian framework. Our university validated part-time undergraduate and postgraduate programmes equip people with the skills to help others.

CWR courses cover everything from how to care for ourselves and our loved ones, to whole church programmes such as *Paraclesis*, which encourages people to come alongside others.

CWR publications address every area of living well – from pastoral care and teaching on mentoring, to equipping all ages to discover routes to emotional and spiritual wellbeing.

To find out more about all our events, resources and training, visit **cwr.org.uk**

SmallGroup central

*All of our small group ideas
and resources in one place*

Online:

smallgroupcentral.org.uk
is filled with free video teaching,
tools, articles and a whole host
of ideas.

On the road:

A range of seminars themed for
small groups can be brought to
your local community. Contact us at
hello@smallgroupcentral.org.uk

In print:

Books, study guides and DVDs
covering an extensive list of themes,
Bible books and life issues.

Find out more at:
smallgroupcentral.org.uk

Courses and events

Waverley Abbey College

Publishing and media

Conference facilities

Transforming lives

CWR's vision is to enable people to experience personal transformation through applying God's Word to their lives and relationships.

Our Bible-based training and resources help people around the world to:
• Grow in their walk with God
• Understand and apply Scripture to their lives
• Resource themselves and their church
• Develop pastoral care and counselling skills
• Train for leadership
• Strengthen relationships, marriage and family life and much more.

Our insightful writers provide daily Bible reading notes and other resources for all ages, and our experienced course designers and presenters have gained an international reputation for excellence and effectiveness.

CWR's Training and Conference Centre in Surrey, England, provides excellent facilities in an idyllic setting – ideal for both learning and spiritual refreshment.

CWR Applying God's Word
to everyday life and relationships

CWR, Waverley Abbey House,
Waverley Lane, Farnham,
Surrey GU9 8EP, UK

Telephone: **+44 (0)1252 784700**
Email: **info@cwr.org.uk**
Website: **cwr.org.uk**

Registered Charity No. 294387
Company Registration No. 1990308